Life Is Out to Get You

Talks on Zen Meditation and Practice

Ray Ruzan Cicetti

Life Is Out to Get You
Copyright © Ray Cicetti 2025

ISBN: 978-1-961043-13-8

Published by:

Blue Jade Press, LLC

Blue Jade Press, LLC
Vineland, NJ 08360
www.bluejadepress.com

An empty bowl is a perfect bowl
because it is always ready
to receive whatever enters it

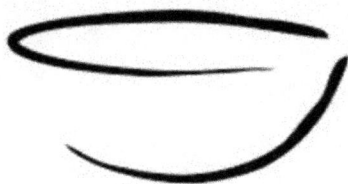

"And the world cannot be discovered by a journey of miles, no matter how long, but only by a spiritual journey... arduous and humbling and joyful, by which we arrive at the ground at our own feet, and learn to be at home."

—Wendell Berry, *The Unforeseen Wilderness*

To Robert Kennedy, SJ Roshi
and all of my teachers living and dead

Acknowledgments

Blake, William. "Auguries of Innocence." *The Complete Poetry and Prose of William Blake*, edited by David V. Erdman, Anchor Books, 1988, p. 506.

"The Uses of Sorrow" by Mary Oliver Reprinted by the permission of The Charlotte Sheedy Literary Agency as agent for the author. Copyright © 2006 by Mary Oliver with permission of Bill Reichblum

"Milkweed" from *Collected Poems* © 1971 by James Wright. Published by Wesleyan University Press. Used by permission.

"Aimless Love" from *NINE HORSES: POEMS* by Billy Collins, copyright © 2008 by Billy Collins. Used by permission of Random House, an imprint and division of Penguin Random House LLC. All rights reserved.

I am grateful to Ed Levy who took the time to not only edit this book, but offered suggestions that were very helpful and made this book better.

To Jacky Fernandez who assisted Ed as copy editor.

My wife Carolyn for her love, support, and patient listening.

To my friend and dharma brother Carl Genjo Bachmann for his unwavering support and to all the members of the Empty Bowl Zen Community.

Foreword

by Kipp Ryodo Hawley

"Who am I?" "Why am I here?" "Why do I feel unhappy?" "What's this life all about?" These are the fundamental questions we all have. Roshi Ray Cicetti has given us a collection of his talks that he gave to real people, interacting with them, bringing up these primal issues. This book format is popular with Zen teachers because it captures the immediacy of the living moment. You feel like you are in the room with him as he presents essential points of Zen in real-world terms and in response to the needs of his audience.

These talks are approachable: Roshi Ray brings his therapist's training and experience with real people in real situations into balance with the meditator's clarity and open heart/mind. He presents his reflections and himself in a way that is instructive for longtime Zen practitioners as well as beginners.

This isn't some place over the rainbow Ray is talking about—it's our spiritual home, where we have always been, and that is necessarily open to everyone. He brings in quotes from poets like Mary Oliver and Frank Wright, all observing this shared life of ours in essential ways, like the sages do. Those sages from the past and present are well represented here, as in, *"We should never waste a good crisis."*

Ray's talks are full of gems of his own, any one of which might be just what you need at that moment to help you see your own life in a new light: *"Nobody cares how wise you are if you don't apply it in how you move in the world."* And *"Whatever your problem, when you hang out with it, when you are curious rather than condemning and are willing to look at and through it, and see what it's about, it becomes a pathway."*

Even words to help us through difficult times like the pandemic: *"Fear is a thought as well as a feeling: I try to embrace it instead of squash it. So, as I was taught, just see it and say hello."*

Give this book a chance and you just might find that pathway to resolving your innermost questions.

Foreword

by Edward Levy

A few months before the start of the pandemic, I found myself in a crisis of my own that led to my moving to Morristown, New Jersey. There, on the second floor of a century-old stone parish house in the heart of town, I discovered Empty Bowl Zendo and started attending zazen. The practice was a refuge for me, and I immediately felt it working to untie some of the knots in my then complicated life.

The basics of meditation were familiar to me, but the way of Zen, and its protocols and rituals were not, and at that time, there was no formal orientation for newcomers. I learned on the job, more or less. And gradually, out of the unfamiliar culture of the Zendo, there emerged an especially warm and welcoming figure, Roshi Ray Cicetti, who gave wonderful and, for me, most helpful talks—many of which are collected in this book.

One interaction I had with Ray around this time stands out. I was trying to convince myself I should take on an additional burden involving a family member, even though my plate was already full. Moreover, I felt I should do this as part of my practice, as an act of compassion. Using a resistance-training metaphor, I declared, "I think I can put more weight on the bar." He paused for a moment and said, "Wait." It was brief, with nothing extra, and in a playful way, spoke volumes to my often futile attempts to do something to make a problem go away.

Roshi has an intimate style and speaks of intimacy often. Not just the deeply personal connection that first comes to mind when we hear that word, but intimacy as an entire way of being in the world. Just as extraordinary closeness with another person blurs the boundaries of the individual self, there is a kind of intimacy that erases our separation, ultimately, from the reality we constantly misperceive as "out there."

This may seem like a tall order, but when you see it reflected in someone's way of being, it starts to seem accessible, an extension of something you already know, enjoy, and take delight in— something you already are. In this way, and in the long tradition of Zen, these talks remind us that enlightenment is found in the intimacy and immediacy of this very moment.

Introduction

About ten years ago, I was teaching at a retreat in Texas when I got a call that my wife, Carolyn, had been taken to the hospital. I immediately flew home and found she was in intensive care, being treated for a blood infection that could be fatal. It was as if the bottom fell out. As I sat with her in that room feeling helpless and having no idea whether the medication she was given would work, I thought about the teaching of not knowing. I understood on a whole new level that this is how life is. We cannot know what will come, or how.

As I sat there feeling groundless, I thought about a koan. *"How do I keep my heart open in hell?"* and after sitting with that, I felt something open inside me, a tenderness or presence that overlaid my fears. The next morning, we got news that the platelets she was given were having a good effect. The doctors felt a little relieved, and so did we.

But it was a clear teaching that we just don't know. Something bad happens. Something good happens. Things fall apart and then come together in some new way. And on and on it goes. But, through that difficult time, a tenderness opened in me. Carolyn felt it, too. After she healed and went home, she experienced a profound gratitude for the doctors, nurses, and hospital technicians who took care of her.

So, the question is, how do we make room for everything life puts at our door? Life presents us with endless possibilities to awaken through the situations we face if we learn how to work with them.

I first heard the phrase "Life is out to get you" at a psychotherapy workshop. The leader was speaking about how we work with difficulties, great and small, as well as the good things life presents.

Afterward, I remembered the movie *A River Runs Through It* and thought, well, that's it. Not only is this life a flowing river running through us but the river is us. As that river, our life includes not only constant change and flow. It includes joys and, of course, suffering.

I think we all, in some way, try to seek joy and try to escape pain and suffering. If you've lived for any length of time, you know this attempt is seductive but seems to only bring more of it. If we are alive, suffering will visit us. The question is how will we work with it? Can we use the experience of difficulties and discontent to nurture our wisdom and compassion as human beings? I believe so.

In Zen practice, we speak of the Way-seeking mind. The Way-seeking mind is like a road or path of discovery we take. We could say it is practicing with the indefinable natural processes of life.

Suzuki Roshi said that the Way-seeking mind means the conviction to fly as a bird flies through the air. Which to me means we enjoy being in this world as it is. It also includes not having to always know. Instead, it is living out the moments we are in. The practice of the Way-seeking mind includes everything. The good and the bad. It recognizes that everything has value.

Another way to think about this is that we all carry with us an energetic presence. When we are connected to this presence, which I would call Oneness, or universal mind, we are better able to manage and use what life gives us because we are open to it even if we don't want or wish it.

If that presence is damned up by dissociating or if we try to turn away from it, we will not be skillful in working with life's problems when they arrive. When we are able to pause, stay with the feeling of fear, anger, or a broken heart and not act out in nonskillful ways, something new can come. One friend of mine called these situations terrible gifts, the gifts we did not want or ask for but accept and can open in us tenderness, compassion, or reveal a new side of ourselves. That is the path of awakening. Life is always providing the opportunity for us to wake up. To return to the Way.

These dharma talks were given between 2016 and 2024. They were offered at our Zendo and at weeklong sesshins and are based not only on the teachings of the Zen tradition but on experiences we as a sangha were going through. This is important because we must ask the question: *What is the value of our practice if it does not meet and speak to the actual lives we are leading?*

The topics and koans covered in these talks, speak to both experienced practitioners of meditation and beginners. I hope they are useful in showing ways to live the great adventure we call our life. I hold in me a deep gratitude to my teacher, Robert Jinsen Kennedy Roshi, and all the other teachers who have entered my life, including Bernie Glassman Roshi and Nancy Mujo Baker. My hope is that these talks begin to give back a little of what I have received. May we, with diligent practice and curiosity, work with life's terrible gifts and difficulties as well as joys and, when they arrive at our door, say, *"Welcome."*

—Ray Cicetti

Table of Contents

What Are We Doing Here?

Good evening, everyone. Last week, a new student came in to *daisan* (a private interview) to talk with me, and she asked, "What are we doing here?" I thought it was a great question. What are we actually doing here in the Zendo? What's this all about? I want to say a little about that. It might be good for all of us to reflect on that question.

What are we doing here?

I think of our Zen practice as essentially about two things. The first is to know ourselves, to find out who we really are. I remember years ago talking with somebody who said, "*You may know what's second nature but, what's your first nature?*" What we're doing here is trying to discover what our first nature is. Usually, we follow what is second nature to us, which are our fixed views and habits. Hardly anyone considers their first nature or what we might call Buddha nature. We are mostly focused on our ordinary life viewed through the lens of our thoughts and habits. We call this the relative. But, in Zen, we are exploring who we are beyond only the relative world. We call this the absolute or essential.

In our spiritual practice, the absolute is emphasized. That's what makes Zen a spiritual practice.

To have insight into the absolute with our whole body and mind. But, encountering the absolute, or the Oneness of things, is not enough because the absolute is not found out in the sky or only on a mountaintop. The absolute appears right here in the relative world. As we chant in the Identity of Relative and Absolute sutra, it's like the foot before and the foot behind in walking. So, what we call the absolute presents itself right within the relative everyday world we live in. It's there when we're having breakfast and talking to our neighbor.

That's the real enlightened mind. It is always appearing and functioning in the relative world. So, this is what we're waking up and attempting to realize. This is cultivating wisdom. Before what is second nature to us, is our first nature. That is our enlightened nature.

The other practice we're doing here is cultivating compassion. So, on one hand, it's about waking up to the fundamental Oneness, or cultivating wisdom—"*Who am I? What's this life all about?*" On the other, it's about compassionate action in the world and in relationships—love in action. Of course, we include ourselves in that. I want to say more about this aspect of getting to know ourselves and discovering who we are.

We go through our life essentially unconscious. So, in one sense, this practice is about cultivating a mind that is more aware, so as not to go through life half-asleep. One of the ways we do this is to begin recognizing our story, the story we were told about how to live life, what is important and what is not. About what has value and what does not. About what is acceptable and what is not acceptable. In other words, about how we were trained to think a certain way and how we continue to live a life based on those narratives. Because the mind forms patterns around those beliefs and ideas, and we carry them forward as if they were true. They form the schema of the mind, we might say. We interpret the world through these stories, perceptions, beliefs, and ideas. It's understandable that we do this; they're given to us when we are quite young, so we can participate, and be a part of the world.

But, they are our specific views and stories, and though of course we need them, they are interpretations of our world. The story is not the reality. The world is infinitely larger than our particular view. The painting of a tree is not the tree itself. What we're doing here is finding out what the thing itself is.

These ideas we have come to believe are what I call the narrative stories. When things change, we tend to hold on to these stories so we can feel safe, comfortable and secure in the world. We fight to hold on to them and try to get others to believe our stories, too. But this creates trouble for us, because reality is not like our stories. The discrepancy between this holding to, or attachment to our individual perception and storylines about life and the reality of life causes us pain. The Buddha taught that this is the basis of suffering.

Another thing we're doing here is sitting still. When we sit still, we are cultivating a quiet but alert body and mind. We calm the thinking mind and open to what exists behind or beyond thought. We're not chasing after any special experience in our zazen. We're not adding anything extra to who we are. We're cultivating attention and training the mind so we can notice the stories without necessarily believing them anymore and begin to look at life in a more spacious way, beyond time, space and identity. I like to say to my thoughts, "Thank you for sharing." We're cultivating a practice of being able to create space so that we don't just track the story all the time, so we can close the gap between subject and object. Our mind creates this sense of separation. I'm here and you're over there separate from me. It seems there is a gap, but there isn't. This is seeing the fundamental Oneness of things. As Thich Nhat Hahn said, "*We inter-are.*"

A very important teaching for me occurred one day when I was a student after daisan with my teacher Roshi Robert Kennedy in Jersey City. We were walking down the stairs, and at one of the landings, he stopped, pointed to a tree outside and asked, "*What do you see?*" Of course, I said, "*It's a tree.*" He responded, "*It's you.*"

So, as I said, what we do here is cultivate a quiet, alert mind. A mind that opens the drapes of our thoughts to see what's beyond them, and begin to know ourselves in a much greater way. We inter-are.

So, we ask the question, *Who am I? What am I?* And we sit with that. We don't assume we already know. We cultivate the mind of not knowing rather than a mind that knows because the mind that knows is going to be closed. When we think, "*I know,*" we've closed the deal. There's no more exploration or questioning.

I remember a psychotherapist, who did a lot of workshops, and whenever somebody said how something was, he would say, "Maybe." He used that maybe as a way of opening us up, making us question, look further, beyond what we think we know.

When I hang out with maybe, I start to know in a greater sense. When we practice what we don't know, we begin to see what's beyond it. Because we don't know, we're actually getting to know ourselves in an infinitely larger way. It's like quickly turning a corner and seeing the sunrise, or a rainbow, and all of a sudden, boom! There it is. You haven't had time to formulate your commentary about it yet. You know the thought about the rainbow. "Rainbows are good. Rainbows are special. I wish there were more purple. What's wrong with this rainbow? It should be brighter, stronger, longer, or shorter. Why don't I see more rainbows?" The mind quickly comes in with all the ways we have learned it should be, and we get caught by them. So, I ask you, what comes before your first thought? Before your commentary clicks in, what is there?

Cultivate the awareness and sense of wonder of an artist who wants to create something new. An artist has to be open for inspiration to come, or else you just keep churning out the same painting. It means being vulnerable, cultivating the mindset of vulnerability. Or, we might think of it as the mind of a scientist, which is always wondering, "*What is this?*" Always discovering and playing with possibilities, perhaps seeing that something is greater than the sum of its parts rather than a set equation or theory or belief that we just carry forward with us.

Happiness

When someone asks me about Zen practice, I tell them it is like a portal we open to rediscover happiness. Not happiness as a mood but as a way of being that underlies our lives. I tell them we come into this world with what I call "original blessing," and in realizing this, we recognize the Oneness of life. We may lose sight of it, but it is always there. Our meditation practice reconnects us to that blessing. It's not that life's storms and difficulties don't still come, but they seem a bit lighter and easier to work through.

This happens as we learn through practice not to incessantly spin off into endless commentary about our situation. I remember Joko Beck once saying that if we have to do something unpleasant or painful, it helps if we notice the extra thoughts we bring to it, like, *"I shouldn't have to do this,"* or *"It's not fair,"* or *"Why me?"* Well, we already know life is not fair. Even the most unpleasant things are a part of our life—they're not extra. Therefore, by dropping those thoughts, we return to the job at hand, taking care of what needs to be done, grounded rather than judging, complaining, or avoiding. This is our practice. We are training the mind not to jump and skitter all over the place but to be open and mindful in whatever we do.

We are training the mind to see who we are beyond the barrier of the ego's dualistic way of thinking, to practice exploring who we are and what this life is about in a more intuitive way. In that exploration, we discover that all things are One, they are all interconnected. We see that we are part of and belong in and to this world and that there is no separate self. We see that our nature is a universal nature. This changes our view of ourselves and our world. We don't endlessly judge and compare. We just do what needs to be done. Our value doesn't increase or decrease based on those things.

As the "Faith in Mind" poem starts, "*The Great Way is not difficult for those who have no preferences. When love and hate are both absent, everything becomes clear.*"

Life takes us up, and then drops us down, then up again. Life is a roller-coaster ride. But, when we have the underlying sense that this is just how life is, we see it as an adventure that includes uncertainty and doubt. Difficulties are part of the journey. At the same time, we practice to realize that fundamental underlying joy.

A good pointer to this is the koan "*What is your original face before your parents were born?*" This koan asks us to expand the boundaries of who we are in relationship to the world. You cannot answer it logically. Try and your teacher will ring the bell to send you back to your cushion!

I remember my first insight as I worked with my teacher with this koan. It was like a flash of awareness. The sense of who I was widened and I realized that everything was me. The maple tree, the bird flying, the man arguing with his wife on the street. I couldn't help but smile with a feeling of happiness. That exclusive egoistic focus on myself as separate from everything else was broken open. I realized happiness doesn't exist outside of us. It's an inside job.

One of the questions that brought me to Zen was

Why—given all the beautiful things in this world, and the gifts I have—do I feel unhappy?

My teacher said, "*You are looking for answers in the wrong place. The answers are inside you and you are focused on the outside. You have some fixed notions of what happiness is and isn't. 'If this happens, I'm happy; if that happens, I'm not.' Who are you,*" he asked, "*before your first thought?*"

Like the koan, he turned the light back on me. I began to see that no one was going to provide the answers I was looking for but myself.

Over time, I began to see that the more willing I was to accept my situation as part of being alive, the less I had to evade it, and the more compassion I felt. It's not that all the situations were now what I wanted, but I began to see they were just part of life. I would ask myself, *"How will you respond to this part of life? Will you work with the parts you don't want? Yes! Because here they are!"*

Practice starts with understanding that life is, as it is. Life events—positive or negative—are mostly beyond our control. As we practice, the mindset that refuses to accept these uncomfortable parts of life softens and the value we put on all of life increases. From my experience and what I have heard from others, sometimes great love, compassion, and gratitude arise out of our discomfort or difficulties. In her poem "The Uses of Sorrow," Mary Oliver wrote:

> *Someone I loved once gave me*
> *a box full of darkness.*
> *It took me years to understand*
> *that this, too, was a gift.*

When we stop expecting things to be the way we want them to be, we find more compassion. We might think, *"Well, I didn't ask for this injury, but here it is, so how will I work with it?"* Then the next-door neighbor you do not like leaves dinner at your door with a note saying, *"If there's anything I can do, just let me know."* We might experience a lot of love and support we did not expect or think we deserved.

You think things are going to go one way, but they don't. So, we work to find freedom and happiness despite the underlying difficulties. The cause of our suffering is wanting something else.

This practice starts on the cushion. We find our best posture, connect to the breath, and acknowledge our thoughts and experiences. If you hear a car outside, just be with that. If you hear a child's laughter in the street, just be with that. Just notice these things. They come and disappear. Just experience them. We don't create thoughts about what kind of car it was or go off into why the child was laughing. We don't go spinning off somewhere. We experience these things and return to our posture and breathing. Otherwise, we have left the reality of the moment, and we're off into a distorted past or fantasized future.

We notice thoughts or emotions but don't identify with them. This is very important. I think about the koan, "*On a withered tree, a flower blooms.*" As we let go of the ego's fixed way, our thoughts and preoccupations soften and quiet down. Our projections disappear, and reality can appear. Along with this, greater wisdom and compassion unfold like a flower.

Some time ago, I read a story about a painter who painted a most beautiful scene. One day a doctor came to look at it, perhaps to buy it. When he was shown the painting, he just stared and stared at it until the artist asked, "*What are you looking at? What do you see?*" The doctor rubbed his chin, looked at the painting from one side and then another and said, "*It appears to be double pneumonia.*" So, this is what we tend to do. We only see the world through our own views and attitudes. The doctor missed it. So, we want to awaken to our life beyond only our particular view.

However, this kind of awakening does not come free and easy. In our practice, we will encounter the small mind, like that of the doctor, of our particular view. We will experience pain in the legs or back as we sit and have thoughts of doing something more comfortable. We will feel bored. We will feel frustrated.

I have seen too many students who leave practice because they think meditation will bring a state of bliss and take them away from their suffering. They bring to practice the same mind state that causes suffering in the first place: *"I'm bored so I want to do something else. I'll try yoga."* Or, *"I don't feel like meditating this morning, I'll do it tomorrow."* Tomorrow never comes.

I understand it is hard to sit with discomfort, but there is a price to pay to find happiness. Who said it should come easy? So, we do what practice requires. This is how we advance with anything. If you want to run a marathon, you don't exercise only when you feel like it. You go out and do it. We never advance unless we encounter the discomfort that comes with change. We follow the path and teachings of those who have gone before us to guide us through. Thank you.

The Practice of Everyday Life

The word *gyoji* means continuous practice. It is also the title of one of Dogen Zenji's essays. It refers to what I call the circle or wheel of practice and means to maintain our dharma practice continually. It is easy to lose this continuous rhythm. We hear a talk, and it touches us or awakens some insight or wisdom, but we can easily forget what we heard. We need to hear things over and over, so the teachings that touch us become like muscle memories.

It is the same when we return to the breath in meditation. When I drift off into some thought or dream, I have my breathing to return to. Our breathing is always right here and now. Feel the breath come in and out of the body, feel the inhale and exhale. Don't try to control your breathing. Breathe normally. Just breathe and bring your attention to that. You may try to notice whether you are inhaling or exhaling, but don't let the mind drift off.

Before we enter the Zendo, we take off our shoes, as if to say we are leaving our busy life at the door for a while. When we enter, we bow, take our seat, and pay attention to what is happening in the here and now. When the bell rings, we pay attention to relaxing the body, even as we keep the spine straight and turn our awareness to our breath, moving our mental constructions to the background and our breathing to the foreground.

As we do this, our body begins to settle down, and our mind becomes focused. We do this over and over, and when we realize we have left the moment that is actually happening, we simply return to the breath. We dwell in the immediacy of the moment.

This is part of the wheel of practice.

When you meditate for longer periods of time, it is natural to experience some muscle tightness or pain. Your knee gets numb, or you feel some tightness or stiffness in the back. The more you focus on the discomfort, the worse it becomes. Rather than getting caught up in mentally complaining, return to the single focus of your breathing. Sending the breath to where the discomfort is may even relax those tight places. Breathing to blend with the discomfort is becoming one with it.

This is learning through our training rather than trying to escape discomfort or difficulty. Because, well, it does not work! Part of practice is to not escape but instead to turn toward and try to open up to the struggle. Why? When we become skillful working with difficulty, it is no longer a problem.

A difficulty doesn't have to be a problem.

This applies not just to physical discomfort during meditation but to how we approach any of life's difficulties. In working with difficulties skillfully, an important aspect of training in the Zendo is developing mindful presence. When we learn to be present with and soften into what is occurring. In this way, we can experience a unity with whatever occurs.

I hold a glass of water or a cup of coffee and I realize it is not separate from me. The same as the air I breathe. It informs me, just as the water I drink informs me. It is part of me. All things are part of me, and I am part of all things. All things exist because other things exist. This is the case with everything, whether we are aware or not; everything is communicating with us. Informing us. Everything is relationship.

It takes practice to see this.

My good friend and Zen teacher, Carl Genjo Bachmann, who co-authored the book *Embracing Life as It Is*, writes that Zen practice is fundamentally about paying attention, letting go of our notions, beliefs, and ideas and being with things as they are. Because when we can do this, we close that distance our mind creates between ourselves and all that is around us. If we think that life is only outside of us or only surrounding us that is a problem.

> *We are life, and life itself is us.*
> *Subject and object are realized as One.*

Each situation challenges us to see it this way. *"Here's a new situation for you,"* life says, *"let's see how you handle this."* It may be a disagreement with your partner, a new job, an illness. Whatever. Life presents us with these difficult opportunities, what I call terrible gifts. This is how it is. There's no escape from it, although sometimes I wish there were!

I'm reminded of a verse in the song "Hotel California" that goes, *"You can check out any time you want, but you can never leave."* All too often, we try to check out rather than work with what life gives us.

It is also important to realize there is no ground to stand on, no foundation. As one teacher said, in reality we're all in freefall. Yet of course we all want something secure to stand on, to be sure of.

More and more, I think of this life as a dance. I ask myself, am I willing to dance with what is coming my way? Or do I fall into the useless trap of trying to escape it or create a different life than the one I have? In Zen, we stand up straight and open to meet the moment that is arising.

I love the title of Reb Anderson's book, Being Upright. It is one of the books we study when preparing for Jukai. "Being upright" is a wonderful way to describe how to meet this life. It takes me back to our posture in zazen. The body is relaxed, but we sit upright, with a straight spine, focusing our attention on our breathing or resolving a koan.

Zen is life, life is Zen. Life and practice are the same. This is the wheel of continuous practice, the rhythm of our life. When it's time to get up, we get up. When it's time to play, we play. When it's time to pay the bills, we do that. We just do it with attention. This is not necessarily easy, because we want to have things our way. We don't want this, we want that. I don't deserve this. I deserve that! Our practice helps us not get caught in "this and that." We drop our preoccupation with ourselves.

I'm sorry to tell you it's not all about you!

It's good to have a practice where—instead of stomping our feet or getting angry because we don't get what we want—we can learn to dance with what life presents. It starts with the breath, and we do the best dance we can. That includes joy as well as suffering. We work with whatever comes.

We say, "Hello, let's dance."

Atonement

All evil karma ever created by me since of old,
On account of my beginning less greed, hatred, and ignorance,
Born of my conduct, words, and thoughts,
Now I atone for it all.

In this chant, we make a vow to acknowledge and atone for the hurts and wrongs we have done or caused. We take responsibility for and integrate how we have harmed ourselves or someone else based on our greed, hatred, and ignorance.

What makes this chant so important is that it asks us to recognize things we have said or done and bring them into the light of our awareness, instead of ignoring, denying, or leaving them in the shadows.

This kind of compassionate recognition breaks open the false image we carry of ourselves and how we want to be seen. We look instead at what is called our shadow side and bring it into the light. It opens the door to see ourselves more completely so we may learn and grow as human beings.

The Jungian analyst Murray Stein recounted Carl Jung's criticism of the myth of the Holy Trinity. Jung thought it was a great mistake not to include Lucifer as part of it because he understood that God was not only light but shadow too. So good and evil must be viewed as complementary.

Reading this I thought, *"God could not create something that was not God."*

Jung thought that to include Lucifer would give us permission to sense and respond better to our shadow side. To bring it into awareness so we can work with it.

This gatha is about first acknowledging our greed, hatred, and ignorance— and then, looking at them mindfully, considering how we can work with those issues in order to reclaim our original intention. To do that, we have to inquire about our words and actions that have been harmful. As the mythologist Joseph Campbell said, "*The hero's journey begins with descent.*"

Rather than keeping the negative parts of ourselves pushed down or unexplored, we compassionately welcome them as part of developing our wisdom. To be aware of our conditioned thoughts and reactions is the very deepening of awareness.

Having the intention of seeing, understanding, and being curious about what the wrongs are instead of judging ourselves for them is important. It may break our heart to see these aspects of ourselves, but a heart that is broken is a heart that is also more open.

So, this Gatha of Atonement or At-One-Ment implores us to look at atonement as a way, to train the mind of practice in all situations rather than judge and discriminate parts of ourselves. This is how we grow and mature as human beings. Thank you.

Deep Listening

I'm happy to be sitting with everyone this morning. When we sit together, even across great distances, we sit as one body practicing together; a sense of community and being at peace can happen. This sense of peace comes by being here right now, with things as they are, and with a sense of joy and openness to the life, we have. Life as it is, instead of life as we want it to be, which is, of course, the source of our suffering. One teacher I know said to suffer is to want something else. Well, we all fall into that from time to time so it is helpful to have a community, a sangha to meditate with.

It's always great being here again and coming back to this practice, reconnecting with its joys and gifts, watching when our mind goes wandering off, wanting something different than what we have and bringing it back to now.

I remember when I first started teaching, I went to Roshi Kennedy and asked, *"What am I supposed to talk about?"*

"Well, Ray," he said, *"whatever is closest to your heart."*

"Okay," I said, *"I can do that."* Right now, what is closest to my heart is something my own Zen community here in Morristown is exploring. It's called a *dharmakaya koan.*

Some koans are about the first insight into seeing things as they are. Some examples are: *"What is the sound of one hand clapping?"* *"What is your original face before your parents were born?"* Or the great koan *"Mu."* These are called dharmakaya koans.

We have been focusing in our sangha on the wonderful question, *"Who hears the sound?"* A simple yet profound question. I love the question, and I love practicing with it. It's very ordinary, isn't it? You don't need to know the special Zen handshake or

19

have some special training. You don't have to be different from who you are or be an advanced practitioner. You don't even need to worry about self-improvement. You can just sit down, breathe, and ask this simple question, "*Who is it who hears the sound?*" It is beautiful in its ordinariness.

We work with this koan in a very simple way. We just sit still and breathe, opening our ears and hearts and bodies to the sound we hear right now. The sound of the dog barking in the street, the heat clanking from the radiator, the passing car, the sound of our own breathing and heart beating. *Who hears the sound?*

When we start to work with a koan like this, there is often a sense of expansion, or a beautiful spaciousness. Our consciousness opens. We just listen. We realize the best part of being alive is the fact that we are here. Just as we are. The world is here for us. The world is here for our own awakening. It is always here to break in, to inform us of who we are and what we are. As I create the world, it is also creating me. Which to me is stunning to realize.

To sit with this question openheartedly is allowing the world to touch you, to inform you about yourself before you try to manipulate it or shift it to what you want. It is the moment before our first thought, before we hear any sound. We drop our labels of Buddhist, Christian, or Jew. We drop male and female, good and bad, right and wrong. We drop thoughts of sound and no sound. We just sit and open our hearts to what is. There is no need to judge, analyze, or compare. We can't do anything wrong. I just sit here and breathe. What freedom! I think this is what brought me to Zen practice in the first place. I can't do anything wrong.

There's another layer of meaning here. A statue of Avalokitesvara sits on our altar. She is sometimes called Kuan Yin or Kannon. The name means "*she who hears the sounds of the world*," or "*she who hears the cries of the world*." She represents compassion that is naturally in us.

To hear the sounds of the world means to hear and listen to the sounds of each other, to listen to each other's needs. We accompany each other as we move through life, without pushing our own agenda at the expense of someone else. We start by just listening, or we might say "*bearing witness to the joy and suffering of the world*" and to the joys and suffering of one another.

We start there. This is true not only in spiritual practice, it is the teaching I received when I became a social worker. We start by listening; it is the first training we get. What am I supposed to do? Listen. What am I supposed to say? Nothing. Be still and listen to their life, their experience. Let who you are working with touch you. Let them know you are listening. Without that acknowledgment, we cannot participate in a relationship. But here I mean a relationship with everything.

Many koans are about awakening to sights and sounds. The crack of the *keisaku* (the Zen stick to arouse sitters from sleepiness or distraction).

Our practice and tradition are filled with stories of people awakening through sound. The monk raking leaves in a garden who, on hearing a pebble hit bamboo awakens. The sound of a distant temple bell. A peach blossom falling. A breeze flowing across a valley. A dog barking in the distance. The world can touch us when we sit with attention, openhearted, without an agenda.

We used to go sesshin at Elberon at the Jersey Shore. I remember so clearly sitting in the early morning, hearing the sound of the geese overhead, the waves crashing against the beach, the seagulls cracking the morning silence. Also, on long retreats at Garrison Institute, sitting zazen late at night, being awakened by a freight train chugging by, breaking the night's quiet. An old Zen poem goes:

> See with your ears, hear with your eyes.
> When your whole being is involved,
> your mind is at peace.

Make the body an ear. Open your whole body and mind to the world. Of course, it's not easy to do this. We want our opinions. We like them a lot. We want to color the world with our own palette. We want our way. We want to believe, *my way is the right way.* Because it makes us feel safe and comfortable.

It's not easy to drop this notion of our small self and ask, "*Who is it that hears?*" "*Who is it that thinks or believes?*" Who is that one? I encourage you to try working with those questions. Now is a wonderful time to practice with those questions. For just this moment, drop your point of view and allow something to touch you and inform you about who you are. Start to see, if you have not already, that the world confirms you.

Through our practice, we can actually experience that. Sit with this question for a while: *Who is it that hears the sound?*

The Practice of Waiting

The Dharma, incomparably profound and infinitely subtle, is always encountered yet rarely perceived, even in millions of ages. Now we see it, hear it, receive and maintain it. May we completely realize the Tathagata's true meaning.

—Gatha on Opening the Sutra

Good evening. This evening, I want to focus on the teaching and value of waiting and patience. In Zen, patience, the ability to wait, has great value. It is in fact an essential quality if we are to understand and explore the nature of mind and the underlying causes of suffering.

By practicing patience, by stopping or waiting, we gain the ability to look into or, as I like to say, be curious about what we are attached to, our expectations, and our conditioning. It is more than just enduring. It is cultivating an active engagement with the present moment. Regardless of whether that moment is positive or negative. We can use the word *equanimity*, which is a state of calm and stability. It is mindfulness of the moment that is actually happening, without judgment. It is being with things as they are.

We manifest that mindful attention and patience as we sit in meditation. Because we're so caught up in the belief we're not enough, we end up striving to be or do something more or different. But as we practice the Buddha's teachings, we see there's nothing to attain, and that we're all right, as we are.

I heard a talk by a teacher speaking about this practice of waiting, which I thought was wonderful. I began to think more about it. It is not something most of us like doing. But we all experience it. It might be waiting for traffic, ordering at a restaurant, for our food to cook, to hear back about a new job. I remembered an experience I had waiting on line at the grocery store. I'm on the quick checkout line with only a few items, and the person in front of the line has 15 items, and she is chatting to the checkout person, then looking for her credit card.

I'm in a rush, and everybody in the line is groaning, making comments under their breath, and I'm standing there, too, waiting, waiting, waiting. I'm thinking and judging. What is wrong with this person? I'm thinking. Why don't they add more cashiers? Why didn't I get on the other line? I'm never doing this again. Why don't they kick her off the line? And I go on, they should, they could, I should have, I shouldn't, all the judgment, criticism, irritation, being antsy, all that stuff.

Or I'm at the airport and I have to catch a flight, and there are delays, and we're all standing in line. An announcement comes over the speakers that flights are delayed, and I'm waiting. I start to notice how impatient and annoyed I become. I'm guessing many of us here have had that kind of experience. You can see the nature of our suffering by standing on a long line for a while. Just watch your thoughts. [laughter].

Although we dislike waiting, it is a part of life, so why not learn to wait wisely. It can be a great time to watch the way our minds work, to examine what we cannot do or have to do. To look at our expectations, impatience, frustrations, and the belief that things should go our way.

Writing this, I thought about a student's talk last Saturday. She mentioned patience as a very important quality of our practice. Patience, a willingness to wait, a willingness to just be, like what we practice on our meditation seat.

I hear some folks say they have a hard time doing nothing, but it's impossible to do nothing. Someone asked me what I was doing the other day, as I'm no longer working full time. I said, "Well, for the last hour I've been watching birds at our feeder."

That's the kind of attention we can always bring. We can pay attention to what is around us. Being still opens a door to awareness even when we cannot do what we would like. We're standing on a corner waiting for a friend and they're late. But, we can enjoy seeing all that is around us while we wait. There are surprises in store for us if we look. I like to say, be curious. When we're able to cultivate that sense of presence, to be where we are and with what is happening, something new and more interesting can arrive.

There is a verse to a koan that says: *When we give relief to the mind, the body relaxes, and the mind is set free.*

When we're waiting, we get to see how we create our suffering. We can watch what the mind does when things don't go as planned. How thoughts can create turbulence and discontent. How we get stuck in the what ifs: What if I'm late as a result of having to wait? What if I can't get where I'm supposed to go? *What if I don't make my flight? What if I can't get the things I need for the dinner party? What if I buy the tickets, but the line is not moving and there are no more seats?* On and on it can go as our irritation builds.

It's helpful to practice quieting the mind and just breathing. Acknowledging but not giving into our assumptions and judgments. Instead, watch the nature of your mind and explore what is. Embrace the waiting experience. Relax the body and mind. Then, there is less anxiety, and the mind and heart open. Life can come in because your expectations or attachments aren't blocking it. All kinds of possibilities can occur.

§

A couple of months ago, I had to get cancer cells removed from under my eye and my shoulder. I was sitting in a crowded waiting room, waiting a long time to be called for the procedure. Some people were complaining to the nurses, when a woman to my right turned to me and said, "I've been waiting so long. How is it for you?" A simple question, great question.

We entered into a conversation. She told me that her husband had passed away and she was sad and didn't know what she was going to do about Christmas. Then she talked about how her children had really been available to help her, and she loved them so much because, though they had their own families and lives, they were coming to visit her.

It seemed strange, she said, but the loss of her husband was also a gift because it brought her closer to her children. I shared with her my experience of loss, and we spoke about how we manage in the midst of it all. We talked about a number of things as we waited. How to reclaim joy and move forward when we lose someone. How folks are celebrating the holiday. What recipes to cook for dinner. We had a startling beautiful conversation. All of this came out of being available while waiting.

A door opened to something that was real and true because we were no longer annoyed that we were waiting so long. Instead, something remarkable happened, other people began to join in. One woman spoke of the joy she has when her family gathers together. Another couple shared that they love to travel. This year, she said, they are going to Costa Rica, which opened up a conversation about bird watching there.

There we were chatting about life. And you know what happened? I forgot I was irritated having to wait. When they finally called me for the procedure, I said goodbye to about seven people, and they all waved to me. Goodbye Ray. Good luck. It was a beautiful moment.

Sometimes when I'm writing a poem, the words come easily, and sometimes they don't. I have to wait. When I do, something unexpected can arrive. I wrote a poem about this experience.

Sitting Outside the Stone Bean Cafe by the Raritan River

As I struggled to find a few words to put on the page,
I was startled by a shape —all determination and wings
that floated between the rhythms of the trees to land
without a sound in the velvet water.
Great Blue Heron, I whispered, to give it a name.
Its eyes bright and wide as a yellow moon.
Its neck stretched high over the changeless river,
still and awake as a monk in meditation.
And like a temple bell ringing me to attention, my breath held in
to stop time, I sprang up to watch it, enchanted, no longer thinking
about my life's drama, the brokenness of this world
where the words I was waiting for will come from,
what I had to do and where I had to be.
And I picked up my pen, opened my book,
and knew exactly what it was
I wanted to say.

Something new can come from the experience of being willing to wait. I'd like to suggest you make it a practice: When you have to wait, think of it as a meditation. Just breathe, relax body and mind, look around at what is happening both inside and outside. See what comes. Let life in. See where it takes you.

The Nature of Enlightenment

People often ask me why, if we are perfect and complete and lacking nothing, do we feel so much discontent and unhappiness.

Yes, we are born whole and complete, but it is also true that as we go through life, we forget or lose connection with it. We begin to feel lost, question our lives, or seek to find that sense of wholeness through causes, things, or other people. We ask, *"Why am I here? What is life about?"* Sometimes these questions bring us to a spiritual practice like Zen that points us back to our innate wholeness and original perfection.

There is a Zen story that speaks to this. A young man asked his teacher, *"What about when someone practices meditation for many years and doesn't experience enlightenment?"*

His teacher answered, *"We are all buddhas from the start. Because of that we practice. We are practicing to bring that enlightenment into conscious awareness. The seed is there in us, but we have to water it. Though it is there, some realize it and some don't".*

This awareness is not an intellectual or conceptual understanding. It is intuitive. What we might call in psychology an AHA! Moment. Another way to say it is we are awakened with our whole body and mind.

As we teach here, when you come for an interview with a teacher (*daisan*) you should try to express your understanding more intuitively than conceptually. Because this kind of understanding or "seeing" is beyond the logical mind. It is seeing or opening the "spiritual eye". It is more of an expression of the heart.

So, when you come into daisan, it's not about telling the teacher your understanding. You can get that from books. If you go into a meeting with your teacher with an intellectual response, chances are the teacher will send you back to your cushion to deepen your understanding more. So rather than presenting a right answer, it's about presenting your insight, your state of being or consciousness.

As my teacher once said, *"You only know what you know, but a koan can take you into what you don't yet know."*

Our conceptual mind sees the world dualistically. That is the barrier we want to cross so that we can deepen our awareness of reality, rather than our picture of it. Crossing that barrier helps us answer our big questions: *Who am I? What is life? What is death? What's the deal?* How can I not live a life of discontent and constant seeking?

It is difficult to accept that we are perfect and complete as we are. It's hard to get our mind around that. But, it's true. If you want an example of seeing that perfection, look at a newborn baby. They are the world, and the world is them. There is no self or other. From the start, we are that original perfection. Perhaps you realize it, too, by looking at a flower or a sunrise. A Zen teacher from the past realized it by hearing a stone hit bamboo. Another by seeing a peach blossom. I think that to return to seeing that original beauty and perfection takes a change of consciousness or a realization.

When we speak about our practice, we are really talking about practice/realization, not just feeling good or an intellectual understanding. We might understand something intellectually but that doesn't change our consciousness. We are so goal-oriented that it's hard to believe we don't have to be more. It's hard for us to believe that there is fundamentally nothing to attain or acquire that wasn't there to begin with.

Our Buddha nature, as I mentioned earlier is not "out there" it's inside us. There is nothing to attain. Actually, the more you search for it, the farther away from it you become.

The central practice of meditation is a process of discovery. Think of zazen as a space we open into where realization can occur. For me, it is not so different from being an artist. You can study technique and look at the work of the masters, but to make art, something else must occur. We call it inspiration. We clear the mind to create a space for that inspiration or insight.

Meditation is like this. It isn't logical or reasonable—we can show students how to sit, take the proper posture, or walk mindfully in kinhin, but no one can take a student to inspiration. No one can do that for anyone else. We all have to do this for ourselves to see it. We sit on the cushion with the confidence that we already have perfection in us. We do not have to try to be anyone special. As the commentary tells us, if an ordinary person realizes it, they are a sage. The essential matter of our practice is returning to ourselves. We start with samadhi, which means concentration or radical attention.

One example we use is that the mind is like water in a bowl. Allowing the water to be still instead of moving it around all the time—bringing the mind to stillness— allows for concentration. It is important to practice to still the mind because the nature of the ego mind is to keep functioning. That is, we are always thinking. It is natural for our minds to create thoughts. And of course, our thoughts and ideas correspond to our conditioning and habits. They go on and on like a ticker tape.

So, we have our practice of breath-counting, which begins to train the mind. We do this to build our focus and concentration. When we focus on our breathing, or return to our breathing when carried away by thoughts, we gradually strengthen our ability to concentrate. We do this practice of concentration (*samadhi*) over and over again, just as we would do when we want to get good at anything, whether it be a sport or artistic endeavor. This brings us back to the moment and softens our relationship to our conditioning and thought habits. We return to the experience of oneness rather than, remaining attached to a thought and feeling separate. This is the beginning of freedom and joy. We experience a sense of boundless connection with our life. As we say, the thought is not the thing!

It is our conditioning that gives the illusion that we are separate. Fundamentally, nothing is separate from anything else, just as each finger, although different, is part of the hand. Let us consider for a moment viewing all things as light, seeing the same light shining on and as everything. We are the light. All people are light. Whatever you see, hear, smell, and touch is made of light. Chickens are light. Your pet dog and cat are light. The tables and pencils are light. Thoughts are light. The neighbor you do not like and the one you do like are light, too. When we forget that, we feel disconnected and discontent. Do you see? If we feel lonely, it is because we believe we are separate from everything else and each other, forgetting that inherent light that connects all of us.

It is in a way, nothing special, yet at the same time, wonderfully special.

When we realize that nothing is separate—that we are the world, we feel more joyful about our life and ourselves. We experience a profound sense of freedom. We feel more love, intimacy, and connection with all things because we are okay just the way we are. As an old commentary states: "*When the mind is at peace, the body is not distressed.*"

A Sense of Intimacy and Wonder

Good evening, everyone. Last night students from Drew University came to the Zendo for an introduction to Zen. They make the rounds of various religious traditions. And as I was talking to them about our practice, I thought, "What do we receive and discover through this practice?"

As I thought about this, two words came to me. One was *intimacy*, which we have an opportunity to experience through practice, and the other was *wonder*. Maybe wonder comes first— wonder, then intimacy. Our practice can open us to an experience of wonder about life and who we are; it can give us the space to question our assumptions, to open to something greater than our thoughts and stories, to be radically curious about this world.

A sense of wonder implies a willingness to be open, to not know. I think that being willing to not know, to hang out in uncertainty, is the doorway to freedom. One thing that to me is beautiful about this practice is the awareness that—and this was shocking to me coming out of the Catholic faith—whatever happened, whoever I am, and whatever is going on in my life, I can never fall out of grace. To use the Buddhist words, it is impossible for me, or any of us, for that matter, to not be in the world of samadhi. What is samadhi? The first syllable, *sama*, means equanimity and *dhi* means Buddha nature. So, samadhi is the equanimity that comes from knowing that Buddha nature or an awakened nature is who we are—that from the very beginning, to use Thich Nhat Hanh's word, we already have that seed of awakened nature in us. What we do here is water and cultivate that seed, to let it grow and blossom.

This can be hard to accept, to really get, because for most of our lives, we are told that we are not enough. But our tradition teaches that underneath all that, we are already the Way. We already have and are Buddha nature right from the beginning.

Now for a Catholic boy, this was wild. Initially, my thought was, I can do anything I want. I can never fall out of the world of Buddha nature. Or, at the time I might call it Christ nature. We can never, no matter what happens to us, no matter what we do, no matter who we are, no matter what we think, fall out of grace or out of samadhi.

You can also describe samadhi as a higher state of consciousness or awareness, or you could say it is a higher state of possibility; if we practice rigorously, something begins to wake us up. We may see that we are more than we have been told we are. Often, the longing to see something more comes out of suffering or loss, or out of fear, or from a nagging question, we cannot resolve that brings us to meditation.

Certainly, that's what it was for me when I first went to see my teacher. I was born and raised in Newark, New Jersey, in an Italian-Catholic family that questioned everything. So, I would ask myself, "*What are these teachings and this practice all about? What's the deal?*" My teacher, Robert Kennedy, is a Jesuit. A Jesuit as well as a Zen teacher? "*Hmm,*" I thought, "*What's the deal with that*[laughter]?" But, when I presented my skepticism to him, he encouraged me to carry it as a wonderful question, a question that, if I could hold it and keep asking it, no matter what was going on, could water that seed in me. So, I carried that question for some time. *What is this all about? What is this life about? Who am I?*

That's what the Buddha's great question is about.

Why is there suffering? Why am I suffering? Why is there suffering in the world, and how do we put an end to it?

This sense of grace, or samadhi, is something you cannot lose. Even if you're caught in some deep, elusive notion, in some difficulty, that's samadhi, too. Great anger is samadhi. You start to see, if you value the teaching, that you lack nothing. Whatever you think or feel or experience or are caught in is also samadhi: The samadhi of anger. The samadhi of fear. The samadhi of great sexual lust or greed.

Whatever it is, that is the seed you work with. This was fascinating to me. To use the example of addiction, those of you who have struggled with that, understand that the addiction itself can be the greatest springboard to insight and growth. What's the first thing you say when you go into the group if you have an alcohol addiction? You say, "I have to admit that my addiction is greater than I am," and you work with that. There must be some acknowledgment of that truth, that fact.

Even if you're caught in "I should be more, I should be better, I should be different," that's samadhi. You can't go wrong. It's helpful to look into it.

A few weeks ago, I spoke about the koan *"The coin that's lost in the river is found in the river,"* which essentially means whatever you've lost, go where you lost it to find it. Don't look for it somewhere else. This koan is attributed to Zen Master Yunmen, who used it to guide students to find the answers to their questions themselves, rather than looking externally. The koan encourages introspection. This teaching is also in the Diamond Sutra. Roshi Kennedy and a number of other teachers came up with a call-and-response version of the Diamond Sutra, which is the one we use here—but if you go to the actual text of the Diamond Sutra, one of the lines is, *"Abiding nowhere, the heart/mind comes forth."*

Hakuin Zenji also spoke to this. He told stories about simple people living simple lives. About the woodcutter who carried wood to the village, took care of his wife and children, and lived an ordinary life. The story goes that one day, as he was working, he heard someone chant this line from the Diamond Sutra, *"Abiding nowhere, the heart/mind comes forth."* And,

35

in the midst of cutting the wood, he had a great awakening. So, no matter who you are or what you do or what your life is about, you have that seed of awakening in you

This is true for all of us. Whether we are paying bills, or being a teacher or student, or cutting wood, whether we have physical or emotional pain, that is the samadhi to go toward. The coin that's lost in the river is found in the river.

When Roshi Kennedy was chosen by Bernie Glassman to become a Zen teacher, many Catholics and Buddhists were upset. They were not ready to accept that a Jesuit priest would also be a Zen teacher. The Catholics would say, "*You have left our tradition, you've betrayed the Church,*" and the Buddhists would say, "*Why are you muddying up our tradition with Catholics?*" I greatly admired that Kennedy and Glassman had the courage and stamina to go forward, follow their own hearts and insights, and teach both Catholics and Buddhists.

Many years ago, when Kennedy went to Japan to receive teachings from his first teacher, Yamada Roshi, Yamada said to him," *I just want you to know I don't want to make you a Buddhist. I want you to be a better Catholic, and this practice should make you a better Catholic.*" That was pretty wonderful. He didn't have to change who he was. He didn't have to give up the priesthood. He didn't have to become a Zen priest. He could keep doing his work. His heart was Catholic—what's wrong with that? But he could do this practice at the same time.

You do not have to give anything up to come here. You can be you. It doesn't matter if you are Jewish, you come to practice. If you are a Muslim, you come to practice. If you are an atheist, you come here to practice. Our everyday life contains the seed of our awakening into becoming more aware of who we are, awakening to that samadhi that is already in us.

The reason I am going over this is that it can be difficult for us to accept. The belief that we are not enough can be very deep in us. It is not true. When you start to practice by looking at your own greed, hatred, and ignorance in an open and friendly way, you see they are the very seeds of your own enlightenment. You start to say, "*Yeah, I can accept that I'm greedy. Okay, let me work with that.*" Hatred? Is there anybody here who has not experienced hatred? How about ignorance? Is there anyone who is ignorance-free? For some, that might be the seed to work with and through. That's the samadhi to work with.

I want to ground us in this, to come to a place of not rejecting any aspect of oneself. When issues arrive, which of course they will, we do not have to have shame and blame anymore. We can look at them and explore them and work with each other, go to a teacher to talk about them, open up to them, acknowledge them, embrace them.

§

Does anyone have any thoughts or questions about this?

> **Student**: I hear you say, "Work with it." Otherwise, it might be understood as, "If you're a greedy person, a bad person, whatever the defect might be, don't change." But I don't think you're saying that.

> **Roshi**: No, no, I'm saying that the change comes through the embrace. The change begins—the transformation begins through the acceptance of those aspects of our lives, not the rejection of them. We cannot look at and begin to change something we don't acknowledge. *The coin that is lost in the river is found in the river.* You go to the same place. We get down. I am saying that the beginning of transformation begins by working with these things. But we have to acknowledge and embrace them first. It's

that RAIN acronym. Recognition, Acknowledgment, Inquiry, and Nourishment. We call forth those things. Whatever the issue, we recognize it and acknowledge it. No shame, no blame. We are not avoiding, we're not denying, we're not trying to kill it. We do not let it overtake us... but we hold it. We say, "Hello, old friend. Good to see you again, let's have a conversation." That is the beginning of awakening. That's the samadhi we're watering. It is the beginning of looking deeply at ourselves.

Student: Thank you, Roshi. It's been, and continues to be really helpful to see how when things come up—fear, anger, thoughts that I would rather not have, feelings I don't want—how I try to get rid of them and to watch how my mind works to keep me from being able to just hold them, instead of telling myself a better story or busy myself to not feel.

Roshi: Wonderful. That speaks to what I am trying to say. You understand that that is the samadhi of avoidance. As soon as you can look at that and say, "*Ah, look at my style of wanting to avoid this, that's interesting!*" Now you've embraced it and you are exploring it, and it opens for you, and then there's growth there. Rather than, "*I shouldn't do that.*" That is going to get you nowhere.

I think this is a very, very, important aspect of our practice. We are not coming here to just veg out, to bliss out. Even though the body is calm, the muscles are relaxed, and the spine is straight, the mind is attentive to experience, and we work with it. Even as we're disciplined and grounded in our posture, we are curious about what's coming up.

That is why I think a lot of people do not stay. They start feeling their greed, hatred, and ignorance and suddenly it's like, *"Whoa, I'm getting out of here. I'm gonna go watch some Jeopardy."*

But if you have the discipline to sit and stay in a posture, following the breath and keeping the mind engaged and not judging, then you may be able to open to these things and start to explore, with intimacy and wonder, the seeds of our enlightenment.

Just Don't Pick and Choose

A very important and well-known Zen teaching from the Third Chinese Patriarch Seng-Ts'an is called "Trust in Mind," or "Faith in Mind." The first lines are:

The Great Way is not difficult
just don't pick and choose.
Neither love nor hate and you will
clearly understand.
Be off by a hair and you are
as far from it as heaven is from earth.

The title, "Faith in Mind." needs a bit of explanation. Faith here means realizing. Mind here means Universal Mind or Big Mind. It is realizing or belief that is grounded in our having a fundamental universal mind. It is not about the mind as in ego-mind. It is Buddha mind. This teaching is the most basic point in Buddhism. Suffering is part of life and the cause of our suffering is picking and choosing. That Buddha mind, being universal is beyond picking and choosing. Beyond discrimination.

Here, trust or faith is not trust in an object. It is objectless faith or trust. It is trust in the true nature of things, or reality. That universal mind I mentioned a minute ago.

Seng-Ts'an is trying to tell us in this verse how we might connect to this Mind. This first line, "*The Great Way is not difficult, just don't pick and choose,*" means don't grab or attach and don't reject anything, and the Way will reveal itself.

Here in the Zendo, we sit zazen. We just sit, keeping attention on our breath, body, and mind. As most of you certainly know by now, we are not trying to attain anything. We are not seeking enlightenment. Too often, people seek out the newest teaching or teacher: Even if we read or are told we have the

41

awakened nature, we do not believe it. We hop from one spiritual tradition to the next, seeking out other ways to "get it." There is an old Buddhist saying that seeking a goal is like trying to catch a feather with a fan. If you want to catch the feather, you must approach slowly and have patience. I think the same is true of our meditation practice, which is a practice of training the mind to be stable, calm, and open.

The Four Noble Truths teach us that the cause of suffering is attachment—grasping and rejecting—and that putting an end to our suffering is being with life as it is. This does not mean we remain passive in this violent, chaotic world of ours. It means we begin with an acceptance of how things are, and then we choose to act in a compassionate way. We have guidelines for doing this like following the precepts as best we can.

This is difficult because grasping and rejecting are so much a part of our DNA. As human beings, we have feelings, fears, needs, physical sensations. It is built into being human and will always be there to some degree. The same is true of discrimination: We discriminate; we must be able to tell food from what is not food. We have our likes and dislikes. It is part of our human consciousness. But, in meditation, we pay attention to what exists *between* our thoughts and desires. We're not going to get rid of thoughts and desires. We just do not want to be ruled by them. Trust in Mind is seeing what lies beyond the discriminating grasping ego mind.

What stops us from realizing what is already there is a wanting to escape our troubles or, as I mentioned earlier, to gain something by seeking it outside ourselves. So, we practice discarding notions of for and against—although again, we cannot do this completely. You can't get away from it. As soon as we speak, we are picking and choosing.

Many teachers tell us to go beyond language and challenge our view. We say, "Show me, don't tell me" as a way to work around the attachment to concepts. In the koan Mu,

> A monk asks Joshu,
> *"Does a dog have Buddha nature or not?"*
> Joshu replied, *"Mu,"* which means no.

The monk must have known or heard that all things, including a dog, have Buddha nature. But as every part of a koan is really about us, he's asking about himself. I have to guess here that though the monk understood cognitively or conceptually that we all have Buddha nature, he had not realized it.

What I like about this young monk is that he is questioning his conceptual understanding. Some uncertainty or doubt is there. This is a step in the right direction because being certain destroys doubt and curiosity about what is beyond our understanding and the wider mystery of reality. As Bernie Glassman used to say, "It's just my opinion. *I don't know*" It is about being willing to suspend what we know and practice not knowing. Because we all live in uncertainty. Our practice is cultivating and trusting that awareness. What we call Buddha mind or Universal mind is beyond the grasping and rejecting. As the author of the sutra Trust in Mind points out, it is found in our everyday life.

We look through or beyond the apparent opposites of for and against or seeking and rejecting. I say apparent because they are very much related. If we like something, it means we dislike something else. This constant attachment to like and dislike, seeking and rejecting, prevents us from realizing our true nature.

So, Joshu's "Mu" or "no" was a way of telling the young monk to go beyond the question, beyond having and not having, or beyond picking and choosing and practicing having a not-knowing mind.

Practicing in this way, we raise our awareness about who we are beyond our perceptions and self-identity and certainty. Now, as I said before, we will always have our delusions and notions—they are a part of life. Anything we think or say is picking and choosing. It's true of every experience we have. So, we ask:

How do we open to this awareness beyond only picking and choosing?

I say it is by looking deeply at the everyday aspects of our life and the situations we find ourselves in. Not just cognitively, as the young monk did, but experientially, beyond the world of yes and no. Beyond grasping and rejecting. Doing so, we realize that everything is Buddha nature. Everything is the absolute. The vast empty sky. There is no separation. In order to see this, which is freedom, we start with trust in mind.

Right Under Our Feet

The real mystery of this life is found in the visible, not the invisible.
—Oscar Wilde

I want to speak about the little things, the everyday things that are also big things. As I was preparing this talk, I recalled how, when I was a boy. I would lie awake in the morning, slowly stretch out my arms, and observe the action of opening and closing each finger in the morning air, noticing my own fingers and palm as if for the first time. It was like this WOW experience for me.

I heard that at the entrance to some of the old Japanese monastery dharma halls is a sign that reads LOOK UNDER YOUR FEET, a reminder, as monks entered the Zendo that the Way was right where they stood and walked. No need to climb a mountain to find the dharma. It's under our feet. If we know how to look, the simplest everyday things and experiences teach the dharma, where we can find insight and joy.

A Carolina wren shows up on our deck almost every day. Although they are common where I live, I never realized they were there. I had never heard their songs, until one day I saw and heard one sitting on a fencepost singing out its *tea-kettle...tea-kettle...tea-kettle* call loud and clear. It was like life calling out to me. Just listening to it brought a lot of joy and feeling of connection.

Wherever it is or whatever we're doing, t here is beauty and wisdom right where we stand.

> *A student asked Master Ichu,*
> *"Please write something of great wisdom."*
> *Ichu picked up his brush and wrote, "Attention."*
> *The student said, "Is that all?"*

Ichu wrote, "Attention. Attention."
In frustration, the student demanded,
"What does attention mean?"
Ichu wrote, "Attention means attention."

That teaching is the little wren belting out his *tea-kettle* call. It is life calling out to us, tapping us on the shoulder to look. Here it is!

I practiced paying attention and writing down what I call everyday dharma teachings. Here's a few of the things I noticed:

The hummingbird at the blossoming trumpet vines in the afternoon.
The fresh shoot of a white orchid at my window.
The passing fragrance of jasmine.
The blue bowl on a kitchen shelf.
The rolling laughter of children across the street.
Amber sunlight beneath white clouds.
Red moss on a garden wall.

I wonder what the everyday dharma teachings are for you.

Everything is waiting to meet us. Life is calling out to wake up to the here and now, and in that moment, there is no before or after. Only the day and whatever your experience is. But we need to pay attention. Even now, the sun on this beautiful day is dropping into the west. Time passes quickly, as do all things.

As our evening gatha tells us:

Time passes quickly by and opportunity is lost.
Awaken, take heed.
This night your days are diminished by one.

I might add to that, "Pay attention."

I heard a story of a young person who went to a monastery wanting to know how to become enlightened. They knocked on the head monk's door and said, *"Please teach me what to do to get enlightened."*

> The head monk said, *"I have a headache. Why don't you talk to the head cook?"*
>
> So, the person knocked on the cook's door. *"Can you tell me how to get enlightened?" he asked.*
>
> The cook said, *"I would, but I'm cooking soup. Why not see the teacher?"*
>
> So, they went to the teacher and asked the same question: *"Can you tell me how to get enlightened?"*
>
> And the teacher said, *"Well, I'm going for a walk in the garden. Want to come?"*
>
> And the young person, *feeling frustrated and understanding nothing about how he was being taught, left the monastery.*

Everything in this universe appears to us in form. The universal is found in the particular, in the momentary events of our life. The call of the wren, the blue bowl on the kitchen shelf. Making a pot of soup. When we pay attention, we find freedom and joy in the little things, which are always trying to open us to that other place found right under our feet.

A Jewel in Bright Light

A jewel in bright light loses its edges. — Zen koan

When I heard the line, "*A jewel in bright light loses its edges,*" I remembered my teacher speaking about the delusion of a separate self and self-centered view. "It is not so important what you think," he said. "What matters is the awareness that we are all that one bright light and how we live out that awareness in our life." His words reminded me that there is a life inside—or perhaps a better phrase is *interwoven within*—the one we usually experience. This was a very helpful teaching for me, and so I offer it tonight.

I think we should be curious about the life that exists beyond the thoughts, theories, and notions we hold. The French poet Paul Eluard wrote: "*There is another world, and it is inside this one.*" Zen teaches we are made of light as Carl Sagan said. But, that light can be covered over or forgotten if we mindlessly go about the tasks of our everyday life of work, family, and relationships. It is easy to think that the outer attachments are who we are.

I recall a talk given by Zen teacher John Daido Loori, who said: "*We look but don't see, we listen but don't hear, we touch but don't feel.*" I think too of the monk who asked Joshu, "*What is Buddha?*" Joshu responded, "*The oak tree in the garden.*" Joshu realized that the eternal or universal exists as each thing. We say each thing is empty. Nothing has its own separate nature. Each thing—like the oak tree—is only made up of every other thing. Water, earth, air. Through meditation, we cultivate awakening to that universal light or consciousness to realize this. We even realize this now through science. The astrophysicist Neil deGrasse Tyson when asked what discovery astonished him the most, said it was the understanding that the same minerals and elements from exploding stars are found in each of us.

49

Life is always trying to offer experiences to wake us up to that, like when we see a newborn baby smile, sunlight illuminating the clouds on a summer day, or we step out the door one winter morning and are shocked awake by the grand silence of falling snow. Suddenly, like a door opening, life rushes in to shock you with something that is more expansive than a thought or idea. We feel more of who we are in those moments, awakened from our dreams into the bright light of Oneness, where there is no edge.

Whenever we have an experience that pulls us beyond our thoughts, we feel a direct experience. It may be a heart filled with sadness from the loss of someone we love or the visceral awe of the sunrise. In those moments, we are like that jewel in bright light, where all the edges and boundaries the mind creates disappear and we find ourselves viewing a situation in a new way.

If I ask you if there is more to you than your thoughts, you would immediately say, "*Yes.*" But we know it is difficult to let go and be open to things as they are. Often, that inner light gets covered over or ignored due to the daily grind of our lives. We forget it is there until something wakes it up.

The practice of Zen is a way to cultivate intimacy. We must look deeply at this—please do not just accept my words and say, "*Yes, how wonderful.*" We must practice opening our inner eye, and to do that is to pay attention. When I say attention, I mean seeing what is there; perhaps "bare attention" is a better way to say it. Because when we pay attention, we feel closer to a relationship or connection with all that is around us. In this way, we are struck with an immense sense of awe and belonging rather than isolation and separateness. The beginning of intimacy is attention.

In *The Art of Loving*, Erich Fromm writes that one of the main reasons we suffer is the chronic experience of separateness and not belonging. He says one way to shift this is to attain a sense of connectedness or union, as we do in creative activities. In the creative act, the person unites with what they are doing, and the material they use represents a world outside. He writes, "*The peasant and his corn, the carpenter and his table, the painter and her picture become one,*" and that process opens us to a greater sense of union because we move beyond our created boundaries.

In the sutra "Faith in Mind," sometimes called "Trust in Awareness," the Third Patriarch writes:

> *To return to the root is to find the meaning*
> *But to pursue appearances is to miss the source.*

and

> *The more you talk and think about it,*
> *the further astray you wander.*

We return to the root whenever we turn and face what is right in front of us. But that experience of union, is felt before the first thought about it. In those moments, the bright jewel loses its edges.

Sitting on your cushion, you have thoughts, and they are usually about the past or future, but even those thoughts are always in the NOW. Our entire experience is only happening now. Someone asked, "*How do we return to the now?*" One way is by opening to sounds, sensations, and forms. Perhaps it is the mindfulness bell ringing or the shout from our practice leaders to "wake up" that brings you back from your thought-dreams into the moment happening. We need to develop a mind that can put attention where we want, when we want.

On the cushion, there is nothing to resolve, repress, or figure out. We just sit with presence, being with things as they are. One teacher said that if you are on your cushion and only having an ongoing conversation about your work, relationship, or the TV show you watched, you are not really practicing. Instead, bring all your awareness to this moment, this breath, this sound, always returning to now.

Meditation is not about blissing out:

> The body is relaxed, but the mind is sharp and attentive.
> We just practice quieting the thoughts, seeing what is beyond
> our ideas and commentary, beyond any idea of "self."
> Opening to this moment, with this breath, this sound,
> there is no edge.

Say Welcome

Good evening. I hope everyone is staying safe. Due to the COVID- 19 pandemic, we are seeing so much suffering and difficultyand so many changes in our usual ways of living in the world.

What's on my mind now is how to use our meditation practice during this difficult time, because what was familiar to us in many ways has shifted. We look out and see the highways, restaurants, and streets empty, people six feet apart, not touching or holding or hugging each other, wearing masks or just staying home. A lot of us suffer being so isolated. So many of us are not able to even visit relatives who are ill, dying, or lonely, having to relate mostly through video chats or on the phone. I know more than a few who have had to set up Seders and Easter celebrations on video.

It feels like the days after 9/11, when we realized our world would never be the same. Now, like then, the world is slower and quieter. I have to say that, for me, after a period of adjustment I've enjoyed a sense of refuge in the quiet, and being able to slow down. I have heard from friends I haven't spoken to in years. They call to say hello. They want to know everything is all right and we have reminisced about our time together.

There is a sense of getting back to or rethinking our values and what is important as a result of what we're all going through.

In addition to the isolation and changes in routine, there is a renewed sense of peace and focus on relating to those around me. When I don't let my fear or worry overwhelm me, I notice things I hadn't paid much attention to when I was moving through the world at a faster pace. A few weeks ago, I went outside to rake the leaves and branches left from winter. I began to feel I could completely be in the activity of raking. There was nowhere else to go, nothing else to do, so I could enter into it completely.

With most stores closed, and not able to go to my office, I began to look at the chores I had to do in a more relaxed way because I had time. I slowed down, and could feel the day. Perhaps we will look back at this time as what one friend called a "terrible gift" in the sense that it has forced us to revisit and reprioritize.

For me, perhaps as for some of you, it seems one value out of this horrible virus is an awareness of the fragility of life, plus an awareness and appreciation of what we *do* have. And, as our practice teaches us, change begins with awareness.

There is a great haiku by Basho about this:

> *Deep autumn,*
> *My neighbor—*
> *How does he live, I wonder.*

I felt in those moments of raking a growing sense of calm, and a feeling of tenderness and wonder toward everything around me. The warmth of my hands on the wooden handle, the cool breeze on my face, birdsong, robins in the yard digging for worms. An even better word for my experience is *intimacy*.

Within this feeling of greater quiet, there can be feelings of fear and isolation. We hear about friends who are sick or have died from the virus. Fear can come on strong at these times. Fear of what may happen—that my wife or family or I could get sick or die. *What if our refrigerator breaks? What if stores are closed and I can't get food? What do I do if I feel sick? What if my wife gets sick? Is it safe to go to a hospital?* We know it's not helpful to live out of fear, to not let fear overtake us, because fears can feel real, but they are not true. It's a fear. Getting caught up in fear shuts down possibilities. So how do we work with that?

When these fears come up for me, I try to get to my cushion, to sit zazen or to simply breathe to calm the energy of fear. Fear is a thought as well as a feeling: I try to embrace it instead of squashing it. So, as I was taught, just see it and say hello. When we practice meditation, focusing on the breath instead of thoughts, a larger field of experience opens up. We relax the body, orient to the moment, and pay attention to our breathing. The tightness around fear or anger can then exist but in a more spacious state of presence. We can recognize and acknowledge our fears and beliefs without getting caught up or carried away by them. This sense of welcoming can transform our fear when we feel lost and afraid and return us to some sense of equanimity.

There is a poem on this theme called "Milkweed," by James Wright:

> *Whatever it was I lost, whatever I wept for*
> *Was a wild, gentle thing, the small dark eyes*
> *Loving me in secret.*
> *It is here. At the touch of my hand,*
> *The air fills with delicate creatures*
> *From the other world.*

When caught by feeling helplessness or fear, I find it helpful to stop and pay attention to my breathing. Because to focus on the breath is to not focus on thinking. I can more easily be with whatever I experience right in front of me without analysis or judgment and smile at it, not letting fear, grief, or anger overtake me. But, as in this poem, see that "whatever I wept for was a wild, gentle thing," and soften to my life as it is, rather than get locked up by it. Be willing to see things from a new perspective and take refuge in our practice, which includes standing in what we do not know. When we can do this, what we can call a third body beyond dualities opens up, just as my experience of tenderness opens when not locked in the dualistic view of this or that, of good and bad.

Here's a short saying from the Ojibway Indian tradition:

> *All the while I am pitying myself*
> *I am being carried on great winds*
> *Across the sky.*

Even as I am caught in the trance of my own narrative, I am part of something larger, something beyond the small self. Practice helps us open up to see something greater, which can lessen our suffering.

I once read a dharma talk that included this koan. A student asked the great master Joshu: *"In times of great difficulty, how should we proceed?"* He answered, *"Say welcome."*

That is what we can do. When we hang out with our dilemma, breathe into it, relax into it rather than react, whether it is a pandemic, fears, or powerlessness, a shift takes place. We stop fighting with what is happening and with ourselves, and feel a spaciousness right in the midst of our issue. We say *welcome* and that is the beginning of utilizing and growing through our experience. We reject nothing.

When we work with a koan, we explore it first from the essential or absolute—that is from a place of not two—of no separation. There is no "over there" while I am "over here." The distance collapses when we embrace our experience, and to do that is the beginning of solving it. When we say welcome to our fear or helplessness, we in a sense kiss the frog so that it can turn into a prince or princess we can love, and bring whatever the truth of our experience is into the light so we can use it toward our growth.

Like the Buddha under the bodhi tree, we make our vow to practice looking deeply, immovable in our sitting, to not avoid or flinch when faced with the realities of this life. We awaken to whatever life brings us right here, right now. We say, *Welcome.*

Awakening

Welcome, everyone. In Zen, we speak a lot about awakening. The Japanese word is *kensho*. *Ken* means to see into, *sho* means essential or original. So, kensho is to see into our original nature, which is our nature.

There is no difference—in the same way that life is not different from our life.

When I came to Zen, I had a longing to wake up. To have an enlightenment experience. It was based on a feeling of personal lack, of my not being enough, and on my believing that an enlightenment experience would remedy that. For me, as for many of us, the answer to my sense of lack was "out there," in some experience I had to have, and the only way to have it was to become someone different. I believed I had to change. I kept waiting for someone to tell me how to change so I could have an enlightenment experience.

Yet, my first instruction in Zen was to just sit and breathe and not believe everything I thought. After a while, I realized no one was asking me to change, be different, or think differently. All they ever said was, *"Quiet your thoughts, sit still, and see what comes. Whatever arrives is where you begin."* No one suggested I change or reject any part of myself.

When I said I wasn't sure I was ready to really meet myself, I was told that was okay, too. I was shocked and relieved at the same time to hear that. I was told to just notice what I was accepting and rejecting about myself and the world around me.

In Zen, this is called resting in the empty field. Instead of being separate from the world, we awaken to a fundamental interconnectedness with it. We begin to see what we want to kill off or remain separate from and how this keeps a kind of Plexiglas shield between us and the world. We do this by continually judging and measuring.

Kensho is awakening to the Oneness of things. It is a realized intimacy with all things.

This may seem difficult to do when we have been busy loathing ourselves for so many years. But it is the loathing or judging that usually brings us to practice in the first place. We are tired of the suffering we put ourselves through. Or, maybe life presents us with the insight that we are more than our thoughts.

Awakening is beyond our control. We can't grab at it. There is no set of instructions or book you can read to take you there. As one teacher said, "*Enlightenment is accidental, but zazen makes us accident-prone.*"

We can help create the conditions that make us more prone to insight. Sometimes, they come out of our pain, failure, grief, or joy. "*The world breaks everyone,*" Ernest Hemingway wrote, "*and afterward many are strong at the broken places.*"

Perhaps it comes out of a genuine embrace of what we disown. Intimacy is unplanned. It happens. And it occurs when we are willing to not have to know. I like to say "Life is out to get you," that life presents us with opportunities to see things in a new way. When we don't have to know, life can touch us and inform us about itself in new and more intimate ways.

There is a wonderful koan about this:

> *Dizang asked Fayan, "Where are you going from here?"*
> *Fayan said, "I'm on pilgrimage."*
> *"What sort of pilgrimage?"*
> *"I don't know."*
> *"Not-knowing is most intimate," said Dizang.*

Fayan suddenly had a great awakening.

For me, this awakening, or kensho, arrived after a few years of regular zazen, retreats, and working with a teacher who would challenge my fixed views.

This laid the groundwork for something that was completely unknown to me to open. You could call it losing yourself. That magnificent surrender to being fully present as you choose to let go in order to experience a more spacious world. To find that takes a willingness to be lost. To stand instead with what you don't know.

The moment occurred when I was reading a poem and realized there was no "I" reading—the world was reading the world. I felt that somehow the world had rushed in to confirm me. As Dogen wrote: "Delusion is the notion that we go out and confirm the world. Enlightenment is the world confirming us." In other words, we empty out all we hold on to about ourselves. Through regular practice, we become uninterested in those notions and more interested in a spacious world we have not yet experienced.

This creates a shift away from the thinking mind. Instead of a past, present, and future, all time is being, as Dogen said, and all being is time. Which reminds me of what William Blake wrote:

To see a World in a Grain of Sand
And a Heaven in a Wild Flower,
Hold Infinity in the palm of your hand
And Eternity in an hour.

We begin to see all time in a moment. The past is a fragmented memory, the future is a dream believed. As we look deeply, breathing and being with what is in front of us, as I was instructed so long ago, we see that the entire world has conspired to arrive here now, manifested in this moment, this activity or thing. And as nothing is hidden, nothing can be revealed. All dharmas are the one true thing. As Dogen wrote: all dharmas are one ultimate reality.

And we are not separate observers of that expression. Otherwise, it's as if we are searching for our glasses while wearing them.

We begin to see that becoming different from who we are takes us away from this realization.

It's about being with. Because it's all here now.

Seeing the One in the Two

Good evening, everyone. I was asked to do this talk as part of our annual Ango period. If you are not aware, Ango is an intensive study time. For us, it will go on for two months. As most of you know, this is a time when we choose one aspect of the teachings to practice. I chose the practice and exploration of love and relationships.

When I thought about working with this practice, the word that came up for me was *intimacy*. What do I mean by intimacy? I mean acknowledging and experiencing what is already present in our life, both internally and in terms of relationship, and not adding anything.

A relationship may be with somebody at work, with a partner, a family member, or a child. Relationship also includes whatever we experience inside ourselves—such as our thoughts, perceptions, and emotions. We might ask, for example, what our relationship is with anger, joy, or love.

Exploring love and relationship is not only about being with another person. It is about being with whatever we are engaged with *in* that relationship. To be fully present with whatever we experience in any of those relationships is intimacy. It means entering a relationship where we don't automatically or unilaterally know or plan what's going on.

Intimacy with all things is living in harmony with them (or at least doing our best to). We become free of our attachment to things when we are intimate with them. The sutra, "Hsin Hsin Ming" (Verses on the Faith Mind) points to this when it says:

> *When love and hate are both absent, everything becomes clear and undisguised. Make the smallest distinction, however, and heaven and earth are set infinitely apart.*

I think you all know and have experienced this in some way. Because the practice of Zen, fundamentally, is seeing and embracing what is there in every moment of our life. It doesn't mean we're attached to those things—we practice to not get caught up in dualistic notions—but we acknowledge them. Also, it doesn't mean we should suppress anger or sadness. It means we note them but don't necessarily act on them.

When we drop those dualistic notions, there is Oneness. Another word for Oneness is intimacy. We can experience that intimacy, that Oneness, through a relationship with anyone or thing. We drop the idea of subject (*me*) looking at object (*you*). When that dropping off of subject and object occurs, intimacy is what is left.

Another example might be lovemaking. If we are fully engaged in a moment of lovemaking, self and other are forgotten. What is left? The experience of love. When we are fully engaged with anything, self and other drop away and there is that sense of being one with.

So, an important aspect of relationship is not turning away from whatever we are experiencing. As you walked up South Street, did you see people chatting, shopping, heading into the bars, walking their dogs, or huddled against the cold? Did you feel the cool evening breeze against your face?

Were you aware of what was going on all around you and inside you? Were you calm, or were you nervous? Were you angry, or did you feel a sense of peacefulness?

How conscious are we about the moment that is occurring?

Perhaps, like me, you were thinking about making sure you got to the cushion on time. *Who else might be there? Who is going to show up and who isn't? What are you going to do after meditation?*

We get pulled into side stories rather than being with what is actually unfolding. Being with what is unfolding—instead of the narrative about what is unfolding—starts with being mindful, paying attention.

Cultivating mindful attention opens us to what is extraordinary in the ordinariness of day-to-day life. I can say, like most of us here, I do not want to live an unconscious life. As we chant in the Evening Gatha: "*Time passes quickly by, and opportunity is lost.*" The moments that pass will never return. Yet cultivating mindfulness is so hard to do.

Remember Roshi John Daido Loori's words: "*We listen but don't hear; we touch but don't feel, we look but don't see.*" It is wonderful to have a practice that brings us back to conscious awareness and intimacy. This intimacy is always available to us. All we have to do is turn our attention back to what is actually happening. What is right here, now. That's what practice is about. It's returning, returning to the moment. Coming home.

It doesn't really matter what the experience is. Happy, grumpy, sleepy [laughter]. Like the Seven Dwarfs. Wasn't it Happy, Grumpy, Sneezy, and Dopey? I don't think there was a Creepy, was there [laughter]?

Intimacy involves a willingness to turn toward your experience. Sometimes we rely on our partners for this. Your partner will often tell you what you don't see. We say, "*I'm not grumpy,*" and our partner tells us, "*Oh, yes you are!*" The person you are with may enlighten you about how you are coming across [laughter]. But if we can return to look at our own experience, then we might say, "*Well, okay, so yeah, I'm grumpy!*" No laws have been broken. No crime has been committed. "*I didn't sleep so well. I'm grumpy.*" Okay, let's be with that.

We start from the teaching of "*being with*". This is living out of Oneness. The practice of Zen is about seeing the Oneness in the two. Because we too often fall into seeing only two.

We practice to try to close that gap, to come back to see both the one in the two and the two in the one, rather than viewing them as separate.

It is interesting to me, and maybe you've experienced it, too: When I'm able to view things or situations as not separate but instead acknowledge them, what happens? The grumpiness, impatience or anger has been transformed, and we're transformed. Because I've embraced it, it doesn't have power anymore. Then Carolyn and I laugh about it and intimacy is there. The practice of this kind of intimacy is about turning toward whatever we want to reject or deny.

Sometimes I want to reject an experience. Let's say I want to reject sadness. Oh, I'll take happiness, but I don't want sadness. We can see where we do that, and so our practice is to then try to turn toward that sadness. To welcome it as much as we can.

Intimacy is about turning toward something to be one with our experience.

This can happen in many ways. We see a sunset or sunrise, and in that moment of awe and beauty, we forget ourselves. In that moment, before the thoughts or labeling kicks in, there is just the experience of sunrise. We feel the intimate connection. There is no "you" as subject observing the object of "sunrise." There is only the experience itself. Oneness.

Sometimes when I'm practicing, I fall into the trap of using meditation as a way to avoid something, to create some altered state, away from the one that's going on. Sometimes we go to the cushion not to embrace a feeling or notion but to try to get rid of it, trying to create something else because we want something else. As one teacher wrote, *"Half the time, we're trying to just stay out of trouble in relationships. We want to be comfortable. And the other half we want the other person to just be or do what we want them to do."* We kind of lurch from one side to the other, he says, which is both funny and true.

We think, if you just see it my way, we wouldn't have any problems, we'd be alright. We'd be happy, wouldn't we? Yeah. [laughter]. If I am angry or upset, for example, I can go to the cushion. But going to the cushion is not about avoiding or getting rid of something. It is more about embracing it, exploring it.

I think many people who come for zazen as beginners are looking for a way out of an experience; they want to create a different one. One that might make them feel better. As soon as we talk about being one with what you have, or who you are, they become uncomfortable.

This sense of intimacy begins with being willing to do our own internal work first. Acknowledging our own limp, our own brokenness. Acknowledging the areas we don't like or judge ourselves for—our greed, hatred, and ignorance.

As soon as you start to embrace and explore what that brokenness is about, you are broken into wholeness. When you go into the brokenness, there is a wholeness there. We might say, *"We break into Oneness."* We might think that greediness, hatred and ignorance are second nature to us. So now, I ask, what is your first nature? We practice to return to our first nature.

We work with this by hitting the pause button, just stopping. If I find myself wanting to reject something, or get somebody to change, or think they should be different or I should be different, I just stop. What I do once I recognize that is to simply stop and breathe. I stop the old narrative and breathe, and wait.

It breaks the trance to do that. It stops the storyline, the train of thought. Even if you have nothing to say, you can put the brakes on by simply stopping and breathing. Even if your partner insists, "*Don't you have anything else to say about this?*" you can always say, "*Actually, I don't right now.*" And they say, "*Oh...*" [laughter].

Once I pause, that opens the door to listening. Because the other goal I've set regarding love and relationships during this practice period is to get much, much better at listening. At embracing your experience as my partner, as my friend, at listening to your experience. It doesn't mean I have to do anything; I just want to be more receptive.

What are your thoughts? What are your feelings? What is your perspective? What is your point of view?

I was reading, Kahlil Gibran, who wrote something profound about relationships: "*Fill each other's cup, but drink not from one cup.*" You can fill each other's cup, but you still have your own cup. We do not lose ourselves. "*Stand together,*" Gibran wrote, "*yet not too near together, for the pillars of the temple stand apart. And the oak tree and the cypress grow not in each other's shadow.*"

A relationship, an intimate relationship, whether it's with a friend or your lover or whomever, is reciprocal, where your responsibility is to help me be more me, and my responsibility is to help you be more you. Then we have a sense of real intimacy, and we have the Oneness but also the two. It is right there.

When we fall off that wagon, which we will, we simply go back to our practice to get back on. Off, on, off, on. In my experience, the more I practice this, just a little bit at a time, the more I'm on the wagon, and I fall off just a little bit less.

This is how I see practice with intimacy in relationships. First, there is intimacy with ourselves. What I mean by this is that everything is Buddha nature, so we open our hearts and look at what part of our true nature we have a hard time accepting. We look at where we create gaps in our own experience, where we want to reject something about ourselves. Then we turn toward it. We bless it. We talk about this in the Zendo when we say that whatever arrives is your true nature, so shine a light on it. Just say *yes* to it. Thank you.

Kyogen's Man Up a Tree:
Don't Waste a Good Crisis

Thank you for inviting me to offer a talk. First, I want to say hello to my teacher. It's good to see you here. I want to say thank you, Roshi, for all you've done for me, and all you continue to do in your work for so many students at Morning Star. I hold you deeply in my heart. You're always with me. So that's the most important thing. Well, there's my *teisho* right there. I don't need to say anything else, but of course, I must.

I want to share a koan I've been hanging out with that has been important to me. It's Kyogen's "Man Up a Tree," from the koan collection *The Gateless Gate*. Let me read the main case to you. Master Kyogen said:

> *It's like a person up a tree who hangs from a branch by their mouth. Their hands cannot grasp the bough; their feet cannot touch the ground. Another person comes underneath the tree and asks the meaning of Bodhidharma's coming from the West. If the person doesn't answer, they don't meet the questioner's need. If the person does answer, they'll lose their life. At such a time, what should that person do?*

I think we all understand that in a dire situation like this, eloquence and knowledge are not going to be of much help.

The background to this story is that Kyogen was a student of Isan, who once asked him, "*Show me your original face before your parents were born*"—a classic Zen question to assess a student's insight. Kyogen goes through one intellectual response after another, and Isan rejects all of them.

Finally, Kyogen says, "*Teacher, I can't find the answer to this. Will you please teach me?*"

Isan responds, *"If I did explain it to you, you'd hate me for it later. Besides, my understanding is my own. It could never be yours."*

Here, as in many teachings in our tradition, Kyogen has come to the edge of something, perhaps a glimmer of a new way of viewing the world or a more spacious consciousness, but he cannot quite cross over into what that is. He exhausts himself—as we all have—with intellectual, logical, and conceptual responses that the teacher rejects.

I love Isan because the heart of our practice is that spiritual awakening is not based on any kind of concept or idea. Life is not a concept or idea. Insight or spiritual awakening into our true nature certainly isn't. It is an awareness we open to, because it's already there. The question is, *How do we open to it?* Of course, it opens for each of us in our own way, which is what Isan is telling the young man. Nobody can give it to you. As far as I'm concerned, if you are ever with a teacher who tries to give you their answer, you ought to find someone else!

The story goes that Kyogen threw away his books in despair and became a wandering monk. He took a job sweeping and cleaning a garden. One day, as he was sweeping, he swept a stone into some bamboo. *Tock.* And suddenly, he had an awakening.

He runs to Isan, offers incense, and bows in gratitude to him for not giving an answer, for letting him find it for himself. That is so beautiful to read. I imagine the scene of him dropping the rake and running to the monastery, pushing himself into *daisan*, and bowing in front of his teacher to thank him.

Let me say a word about how this relates to meditation. I think it's helpful to approach meditation practice like a poet or an artist. The way of the artist is not logical or conceptual. Maybe some of you have an art practice, which I highly recommend as a way to orient to a more intuitive rather than logical self. In meditation, we practice opening up our experience to something greater than what we know—just like the artist opening to creativity. We open to something more experiential. Often, we call this having a "*don't-know*" mind. We cultivate a way of being with what we don't know. Like the artist, we sit with attention, waiting for inspiration to come.

I have a friend who is a painter. She lives in South Jersey. She told me that sometimes when she paints, she disappears. She said there is just the action of painting itself. There is just the movement of the brush. Any gap between her and the canvas closes. She is just painting, fully present in that moment. This is intimacy. This is Oneness in an experience. No self, no other. I think this is what happened when Kyogen swept. He forgot himself. When he heard the *tock* of stone against bamboo, he heard it as if for the very first time. He connected to something greater than what he knew. It was an *aha* moment of insight, we might say. This is what can occur for us as well. We close the gap between ourselves and our life. We open to a greater consciousness.

You hear a birdsong every day, or a child's laughter, but one day you hear it as if for the very first time. For Kyogen, it was pebble hitting bamboo.

Now, it is also true there is value in reading and studying texts. That, of course, is another important part of practice. To read. To learn. So, there's nothing wrong with intellectual pursuits. It can be valuable to do that, but I suggest there's a way to study. Maybe we read from the belly. Maybe we read from the breath instead of the head. A Zen teacher who is also a friend describes it as "*the body reading.*"

Read a line or two and then stop and breathe. Breathe in and then read another line or two and then wait and breathe and pause and take it in. Let each word open you.

§

In so many of the koans we study, there seems to be a crisis that can bring us to a new awareness. That is what I think happened with Kyogen. A teacher said, *"We should never waste a good crisis."* I like that. We are all like Kyogen hanging by our teeth. This is life, so, we should use crises as best we can. Something happens that overturns our set ways of seeing things or moving in the world, that makes us question who we are or makes us wonder about the way we have looked at the world. Which is another way of saying we are outgrowing some small idea that we have held.

Kyogen starts to look at himself much more deeply. I'm guessing he just emptied himself into sweeping, embracing the life that he had instead of the one that he wanted. On hearing just this sound of a stone hitting bamboo, it became clear to him. For us, it might be the crash of an ocean wave, or the sound of the bell. Perhaps the sweep of the wind across your face.

Being one with what we're doing. Like my artist friend who was so intimate, so one with painting that she forgot herself. What a beautiful thing. Now, this is not easy to do. We have our emotions and conditioning to deal with. But it is important to remember that Kyogen's situation is how it is. Like him, we are all hanging in some way. There is no ground to stand on. There is no place to hold on to.

We all long to have life be the way we want it to be or should be. We have our beliefs, addictions, and attachments. What I am saying may be simple, but it's not easy. It takes practice. It takes consciousness and rigor, I believe, a rigor in practice, as with any art.

Kyogen's awakening reminds me of the 10th ox-herding picture, the image in which a young man is happily riding the ox down the road with a bundle on his back. He is at peace. Kyogen's awakening can happen for us, too. Happily carrying our life's bundle, riding on the ox of our true nature. Life just as it is. Always changing, shifting.

I'm guessing that the crisis for Kyogen after leaving Isan was the same as any crisis for us—old age, arthritis, failing at something important, loss of a friend, divorce—whatever it may be. If you live long enough, you understand life will break your heart. We have a practice that helps us to meet crisis when it comes. As I said, there is no set ground to stand on. We are all hanging from a branch in some way. This is how life is.

What we can do is meet our life with an open heart. Never waste a good crisis because when we know how to acknowledge situations we hadn't planned on, when we know how to practice in this crazy, changeable life by quieting the mind, it changes us and opens us. We don't hold on to the old ways of operating anymore.

This is difficult but important. If you are hanging from whatever your branch is, whatever that may be, that crisis can be an opportunity, a moment when Zen expresses itself. Zen manifests in the crisis itself. Zen manifests in whatever it is that we are doing. There is nothing like a good crisis to awaken us. Thank you.

Aimless Love

This is the last day of our retreat so we gather and begin to integrate whatever we have discovered for ourselves, whatever awareness or insight has brought, not only to understand why we suffer but also to discover how we can love more, how we can live a happier and more joyful life.

Nobody cares how wise you are if you don't apply it in how you move in the world. To have love and compassion in your life for other people, and for yourself.

Hopefully, something comes to us in the time we are sitting. Zazen should not be a blank slate. The body is relaxed, but the mind is attentive, it is alert, not passive. In the sitting that we do over a period of time, we can discover the cause of our suffering. Then the most important thing is what you do when you get up from your cushion and how you apply these discoveries in your life. Otherwise, what is the point?

We start by recognizing the things we attach to because they turn us away from life, away from love—from actual love. They turn us away from actual relationships. They turn us toward how we would like things to be, not how they are.

The practice of understanding what makes us suffer, and how we discover more love and intimacy, starts with attention, with cultivating what we could call Buddha Mind or the awakened mind—I call it a mind of wonder, of curiosity, a deep curiosity about things, assuming nothing. What we know is so small and what we do not know is so vast. We can put what we know in a little satchel and carry it around with us. That knowing can make us feel very comfortable; we all want to be loved, to know, to be smart, and we all want to have the right answer. That is always with us, but you don't have to fall in love with it. When we put that satchel down and turn our attention to the vast world out there, we become more aware of what we do not know.

This is not so easy to do. We have our preconditioned ideas of what we want and a belief that knowing serves us better than not knowing. But, knowing shuts down curiosity. Believing we already have answers closes the curious mind. A closed mind is not open to possibilities. Our practice is about dropping all that and turning toward what we do not know. That is, cultivating a mind of wonder. Go out into the night sky and look up at the stars and infinite spaciousness. You'll have a much greater sense of what you don't know. Be curious about that. Enjoy that.

You are not going to suddenly get rid of your preconditioned notions, your concepts and ideas and old patterns of relating. But, you do not have to live them out for your whole life, either. What we do in zazen is begin to recognize them, to see them. We don't give them all our attention, because they keep us in a very narrow place of awareness.

As I tell the folks in our Zendo, "*Just say hello to them.*" I like to say "*Good to see you, old friend. Here you are, back again to visit me.*" We tell them "*Have a nice day.*" Then we turn our attention to something that we really don't know and have a deep curiosity about. What we want to do is open up our sense of wonder and curiosity.

A phrase that has been a favorite of mine is "life is out to get you"—life is always trying to break us open, to awaken us.

Life gives us something we did not plan for, that we never intended, and yet here it is. So, the question becomes, how will you turn to that, how will you utilize that experience, those things in your life that are coming?

During the pandemic, some people said, "*This COVID virus is horrendous, it's horrible,*" and it was, and we did what we had to do to take care of ourselves and mourn what was lost. At the same time, I noticed acts of love, generosity and caring. I don't think would have happened had it not been for the virus. It is not about trying to get the life that you want but living the life that you have.

My question to all of us is, "*How do we utilize what we have? How will we respond?*" We open up this great question of not knowing and being able to practice not knowing.

One of the first times I went into daisan with Roshi Kennedy, he asked, "*So what do you want?*" I said, "*I want to wake up to life.*"

He said, "*Okay.*" Without another word, he raised his teaching stick. He held up his teaching stick and asked me, "*What is this?*"
"*Well, it's a stick.*"
"*No, it's not a stick.*"
"*Okay, fine, then it's a piece of wood.*"
"*No, it is not a piece of wood.*"
"*Then it's obviously a part of a tree.*"
"*No, it's not a part of a tree.*"
We went on and on like this, four or five times, until I said,
"*Okay, I give up, I really don't know what it is.*"

He said, "*Good, that is where we begin our practice.*"

I left with a sense that something was possible here. I had no idea what it was, but I was curious about it. He wasn't just giving me a hard time. There was something beyond my labels, names, and concepts about things that I knew he was trying to show me. I carried that with me for a long time.

He introduced me to a greater sense of who I was and what was possible in the world. I offer that teaching to you. That it is much more interesting to be curious about life than to have an answer.

There is a poem, "Aimless Love," that I feel expresses this teaching. If you have read it before, relax and read it now as if for the first time. It is one of my favorites by Billy Collins.

This morning as I walked along the lake shore,
I fell in love with a wren
and later in the day with a mouse
the cat had dropped under the dining room table.

In the shadows of an autumn evening,
I fell for a seamstress
still at her machine in the tailor's window,
and later for a bowl of broth,
steam rising like smoke from a naval battle.

This is the best kind of love, I thought,
without recompense, without gifts,
or unkind words, without suspicion,
or silence on the telephone.

The love of the chestnut,
the jazz cap and one hand on the wheel.
No lust, no slam of the door—
the love of the miniature orange tree,
the clean white shirt, the hot evening shower,
the highway that cuts across Florida.

No waiting, no huffiness, or rancor—
just a twinge every now and then

For the wren who had built her nest
on a low branch overhanging the water
and for the dead mouse,
still dressed in its light brown suit.

But my heart is always propped up
in a field on its tripod,
ready for the next arrow.

After I carried the mouse by the tail
to a pile of leaves in the woods,
I found myself standing at the bathroom sink
gazing down affectionately at the soap,

So patient and soluble,
so at home in its pale green soap dish.
I could feel myself falling again
as I felt its turning in my wet hands
and caught the scent of lavender and stone.

Continuous Practice

Welcome, everyone. I want to say a few words about the great essay by Dogen called "Continuous Practice." It teaches what we speak about so often here: that life is practice, and practice is life. Dogen wrote this essay in the 13th century and became one of the most influential thinkers and teachers in the Buddhist tradition. The first paragraph goes:

> *On the great road of Buddha ancestors, there is always unsurpassable practice, continuous and sustained. It forms the circle of the Way and is never cut off. Between aspiration, practice, enlightenment, and nirvana, there is not a moment's gap. Continuous practice is the circle of the Way.*

While it's true that an enlightenment experience can change how we see, relate, and live, it is also true that insight or enlightenment is not different from actual practice. As Dogen teaches us, rather than enlightenment experience being an unobtainable distant goal, that experience is found in any moment of practice. A moment of zazen is itself the enlightened way. All the stages of practice are happening at once.

What Dogen is teaching us here may be difficult to accept given the beliefs and narratives we have been taught—that we are not good enough or smart enough, or whatever it is—we are not enough.

We are so conditioned by our well-oiled beliefs that it's hard to accept we can be free of them. It may be hard to accept that the spiritual practice of zazen is more about undoing these beliefs and perceptions than it is about instructing us to do more, be more, or to be better or different than we are. The notion of not being enough can be so engrained we miss how rare and wonderful our life is. We do not consider this very often—that being human is a gift and there is no one in the world like us. To realize this, we take up the practice of the Great Way, the great road of liberation.

As Dogen tells us in this first paragraph, the Way is also a circle. A circle doesn't go anywhere. It goes round and round. It keeps returning to where it started, just as we keep returning to our practice of zazen—yet each returning is different.

It is like time. Time does not go forward. It is always here— now. And in the next second, here now again, yet new.

Although we think of time in a linear way, time is not linear. In our practice of zazen, we are always returning to Now! Now is where we are. Every step we take is returning home to where we are…and each return is different.

Dogen is telling us that the initial aspiration for practice, the practice itself, the insights arrived at, and living them out in our life are all going on at the same time. "There is not a moment's gap." All moments are contained in one moment.

Take a moment to reflect on this. This is the circle of the Way. Every effort we make includes the entire path of practice. As Dogen says: *"As soon as we sit, enlightenment is there."* Each step on the path is the entire path. The reality of this gets lost due to our worries, beliefs, and misperceptions. But life, and doing our best to live it fully with an open heart, is the practice. If this seems strange, it might help to remember that there is more going on in this world than we perceive. As we say in the jukai ceremony, life is subtle and mysterious. We should question our perceptions.

Dogen says: *"This being so, continuous practice is unstained, not forced by you or others. The power of this continuous practice confirms you as well as others."*

We have a discriminating consciousness, which sees things dualistically. At the same time, we have the option to look more deeply. On one level, we can safely say a stack of wheat is not a loaf of bread or soil is not a flower. But, looking with a deeper view, they are united. They are one. Each thing is contained within another. No soil, no flower. Within the flower, the soil is there, and within the bread is the stack of wheat.

Something exists beyond the way we think, feel, and perceive.

We practice to cultivate a mind that not only sees things as separate but sees as well that they are united, undivided, or we might say, interconnected. On this path of practice Dogen is laying out for us, we stop our spiritual seeking and grasping and open instead to our deeper consciousness, which is always available right here. Now. Our life is our practice, not an add-on. The most beautiful sutra is the sound of the ocean or the song of the robin. Zazen might seem different from our everyday life but it is not.

He continues:

> . . . *Continuous practice is the circle of the Way. This being so, continuous practice is undivided. Not forced by you or others. The power of this continuous practice confirms you as well as others. It means your practice affects the entire earth and the entire sky in the ten directions. Although not noticed by others or by you yourself, still, it is so.*
>
> *Accordingly, by the continuous practice of all Buddhas and ancestors, your practice is actualized, and your great road opens up. By your continuous practice, the continuous practice of all Buddhas is actualized, and the great road of all the Buddhas opens up. Your continuous practice creates the circle of the Way. By this practice, Buddhas and ancestors abide as Buddhas. They have Buddha Mind. They attain Buddhahood without anything being cut off.*

By the continuous practice of all Buddhas and ancestors, your practice is actualized, and the great road of all the Buddhas opens up.

Your continuous practice creates the circle of the Way.

This stunned me. Every time I read it, I am blown away. I sat with this a long time, and here is how I see it now. When we first start to practice Zen, we think we are the ones doing it. And in some way, when we first start practicing, we are. We think sometimes we're doing it alone and just for ourselves. It is okay to start that way.

If you keep practicing, your awareness and consciousness expand, and you may realize that you are actually practicing with others. Your practice improves because of others' practice, and you, by your practice, help others practice. You do not really practice alone.

You're doing something with others.

After another period of time, you realize that you are not just sitting for yourself and you're not just sitting with others. You are sitting *for* others and everyone else is practicing with and for you.

This is the Circle of the Way.

We practice with those who have gone before us as well. When I read this, I had an inspiration about the Ancestors' Table by the front door of the Zendo. I thought of the movie *Dead Poets Society*, where Robin Williams stands his students in front of the pictures of those who have gone before at the school. He turns to his students and says they're here now, they're all right here, and then whispers, "*Seize the day*," as if those who have passed are imparting the message to live one's life fully.

When I look over at the Ancestors' Table, I have the thought that each one of them is saying that to us. *Seize the day.* Don't waste time. Look deeply into your life. Dogen uses the words *Buddhas* and *Ancestors*. These are the teachers who have passed this practice on. The most recent for us are Bernie Glassman Roshi, Shunryu Suzuki Roshi, Taizan Maezumi Roshi. That's why the Ancestors' Table is by the door when you first come in.

This practice is both personal and universal. When we bow to our cushion and we take our places, they're there with us, bowing as well. We say here that the point of Zen practice is to become ourselves. I hope that's what you're doing on the cushion, practicing to become yourself in the fullest way.

We have to thank them for pointing the way for us. You can't say that you sit here alone. Everyone who has got you to this cushion is sitting here with us now. Not just teachers. I don't think I would be here on this cushion without my wife, without my dad, without other teachers and other students who have practiced with me and supported me. Even those who have hurt you the most have had something to do with getting you to this cushion. To this practice. We should bow to them, too, because they are here with you as well.

Dogen says that we should thank them.

Dogen writes in this section that the reverse is also true, that the Buddha, the teaching, and the teachings of the teachers before us also depend on us. This is also the circle of the Way. If it goes one way, a circle goes the other way. Our practice illuminates their practice. We practice well and their practice does not die. What they taught does not die. What they did does not die because of our practice today. The circle of the Way.

How can you say you practice alone?

They come alive when we make an effort, and when we make an effort and practice well, it is a way to not let them die and not let their teachings die.

Dogen goes on:
> *Because of this practice, there are the sun and moon, and stars.*
> *Because of this practice, there is the great earth and the open*
> *sky...Because of this practice, there are the four great elements*
> *and the five skandhas.*

Eye, ear, nose, tongue, body, mind, all here, present today, as well as the sun and the moon and the sky and the great earth.

Now that continuous practice is not something people of this world necessarily love, but it should be the true place of return.

Isn't it beautiful that this practice we do is a refuge that we can return to when we get lost, when we don't love it, when we don't love our life, when we don't love anything else. We have a practice to return to, to get us right, to remember, and bring us back into balance.

That should be the place, the true place of return for everyone. Because of this continuous practice, all the Buddhas of the past and the present and the future are actualized when we practice to actualize ourselves. The sun, the moon, and the stars depend on our continuous practice. I cannot think of something more beautiful than that.

Dogen is not talking dualistically or conventionally. He's not saying the sun is shining on us or that we are affected by the sun. He is saying, not just metaphorically, but in reality, when you sit, everything is sitting with and as you. When you are doing zazen, everything—the sun, moon, and stars —is practicing too. Nothing is excluded. I would add if you don't see it that way, you're playing small.

Dogen then goes a little bit further and says the blossoms opening and the leaves falling right now are the actualization of your continuous practice. You realize how grand and how universal he sees all of us. Where do we begin and end, really? He says even polishing a mirror or breaking it is a continuous practice.

He goes on:

> Continuous practice is unstained. It's undivided. It is not limited physically or conceptually. Yet it is fully expressed in and by this physical world. So, there's nothing that you can do, nothing that you can say, nothing that you don't do, nothing that you don't say that is left out. The continuous practice of the Way is all inclusive.

Dogen is not talking about cause and effect. He's talking about universality. He is talking about Oneness. When you stand up, the moon and the sun and the stars and the great earth all stand up together. The sun, the moon, and the stars are already continuously practicing. They are practicing the Way. The great circle of the Way is being here now. Dogen doesn't care whether you see it or not. It is occurring anyway. Because of this fact, you may at some point open your eyes to it.

I would say life is out to get you. Life is always trying to get you to wake up. To see who you really are. At every turn, life is out to get you.

I thought I was this way, but I am that way. I thought it was going to go this way, but it goes that way. I thought she was going to do this, but then she did that. I thought it was going to

89

look like this, but nope, it is looking more like that. What do I know? Life is out to break us open all the time.

Continuous practice, Dogen says, "*Is a practice that actualizes itself. It is no other than your practice right now.*"

Now he says, "*Does not come and go.*"

It does not enter or depart, does it? Even the word *now,* he says, does not exist separately from your continuous practice. This being so, your continuous practice this day is the Buddha seed and the practice of all the Buddhas for all eternity.

All Buddhas are actualized and sustained by your practice.

Every inhale, every exhale, every step is universal and everything is moving with you all the time.

When I was sitting with this at home, it really changed for me. I started to realize that whatever activity I did, I wasn't doing alone, and I wasn't just doing it for me. That everything was happening continuously, occurring all the time, simultaneously. That my practice informs everything, and everything is informing my practice. Man, did I wash some great dishes. I washed the dishes like really, really, really, well. Carolyn was impressed. She applauded how well and how clean those dishes were! (laughter) I vacuumed really, well, because everything, the whole world was vacuuming with me, and it was all right.

Dogen ends this section by saying that even when we fall into forgetting, we have a practice. Even when we fall into forgetting, we have sangha mates to help us return to it.

He doesn't say sangha mates—that's me. He tells you not to think that your treasure is elsewhere. It is right here in your home.

"Wandering around through the wind and the water, you put your life at risk."

Isn't it true?

This is the second and third part of Dogen's essay, "Continuous Practice." He's clear and straight ahead with what he's offering us. I recommend that you read it, study it, and sit with it.

Heart-Mind

Good evening. For those of you who may not know or haven't been here for a while, we are studying what are called the ox-herding pictures.

Now the ox-herding pictures are teachings about the stages of spiritual awakening, and we're exploring and offering talks on each one of them. However, these insights and experiences do not happen in stages. Instead, I would say the process of awakening is more circular, but looking at these in stages can be a helpful way to understand and talk about it.

Last week, the dharma talk was on stage three, "*Getting a Glimpse of the Ox.*" Tonight, we are exploring stage four, "*Catching the Ox.*" The ox is your true self, your true nature. Not your personality, but personality plus. What I mean by that is seeing beyond just the image or name of who we are. Beyond the thoughts and the beliefs we hold. There's a verse that goes with this step of catching the ox:

> *Through extraordinary effort, you seize the ox.*
> *Still, its will is forceful, and its body is spirited.*
> *Sometimes, it runs into the mountains,*
> *other times, it disappears into the mist.*

Roshi John Daido Loori, who was the senior teacher at Zen Mountain Monastery, pointed out that this stage of awakening is about a relationship that includes great determination and intimacy. At this stage, we have an experience of our true self. We realize it and feel it in our body, mind, and heart.

In the commentary on the fourth stage, it says you grab or lasso the ox. There is an experience of being awake to your true self. You are not seeing it as just an intellectual idea; you actually have an awakening to it. We can say it is like an *aha!* experience.

A Zen priest named Ikkyu wrote something that captures this stage beautifully. He said, *"With just one glance at the figure of our original nature, standing here, you fall in love."*

You feel it inside of you like love. I remember the first feeling of falling in love with my wife. I didn't know what to do. I was stunned. All reason fell away. What I felt made no sense. It was a new way of seeing the world, although it was the same world.

I felt overwhelmed, my heart broken open into something greater, my sense of self, dissolving. Opening to something that has always been there but you never really quite felt.

You got a glimpse of it, but now it's in us and is us. How beautiful. Seeing it is like falling in love when we realize we are fundamentally connected to everything. In addition to calling this our true nature, we can also call it a fundamental heart-mind connection.

Heart-mind. What do I mean by that? Heart-mind is a way of saying that the heart and the mind are unified. When you have this experience of Oneness, of that connection, there is an alignment or unity that takes place between the head and the heart. At that point, we feel the value of wanting to continue to practice because we experience something opening inside, like love, as opposed to just another idea or thought.

The great Zen teacher Hakuin said something about this. He said, *"Listen, listen. From the very beginning, you are Buddhas."* From the very beginning, we have this awakened nature, but we forget. We lose touch with it. At this stage, you see that your true nature is pulsing in you and through the world. As we say, *"You are that."*

At times, it may still hide from us. It comes and goes. As the verse goes:

Its will is strong.
Sometimes it heads off into the mountains or into the mist.
You can quickly lose connection to it.

At this stage, you see it, feel it, but you cannot hold it. It heads off into the mountains on you. But you have, perhaps for the first time, come face to face with it. When we do, it changes us. It changes how we see who we are.

This is intimacy, rather than seeing the world of people and things as out there and ourselves as over here—the delusion being that we're the subject and out there is the object, that we and all other things are only separate.

Intimacy means we start to see the unity of all things. That whenever I see you, I see me.

There is no "out there." There is no separation. As the wonderful teacher Thich Nhat Hanh used to say, we *inter-are*.

As I mentioned earlier, this awakening can also be called the heart-mind connection. We realize and experience the unity of heart and mind. When the mind is not in connection to the heart, all kinds of problems can happen. The mind of thought without the heart is a closed fist. It wants sameness. It wants comfort, control, and security. When you connect it to the heart, it begins to open.

The mind without the heart is closed. The mind without the heart can become tyrannical. The mind without the heart can become authoritarian. It thinks, "*It's all about me.*"

The mind without the heart can become lazy, more interested in comfort than curiosity. It wants information over wisdom. It is not interested in relationship or compassion. It views interactions and relationship primarily as transactional. It looks at the world—not just at people, but at things, the ocean, the trees, the clouds, the sky—through the eyes of delusion. The mind without the heart serves only itself.

I remember Bernie Glassman talking about this. Bernie was a wonderful Zen teacher. He tried to address this disconnection of heart and mind by setting up "street retreats." He said to students, "*Please join me on the streets.*" Why did he want to take people on a street retreat? If you go on the street and all you have is five bucks, you have an experience of seeing what it's like to be homeless. To live on the street. It widens our experience.

The point of it was to blur this separation between how we live and how other people live. To make it more porous so that we could feel what other people were experiencing and be cracked open. As I like to say, life is out to get you, to wake us up. When the heart is cracked open, new things can happen. We blossom like a flower.

Some people said this is not Zen, "*What are you doing, man? You're not going to really ever know what it's like to be homeless.*" That was true but it got people to experience something beyond themselves. To step beyond their comfort zone.

You had to go ask for food.
You had to sleep on the street or at a shelter.
You had only a few bucks on you,
You had to make the best of it.
You slept on benches or in a park,
You had to rely on others.

He wanted to help people awaken. To take Zen practice into the street. To show that social action and Zen practice were not separate. Now, we can also call this heart-mind, *kensho*— seeing into our nature. I call it a *"perfect view."*

This is awakening. It's a unified view, a perfect view. But at this stage of awakening, it's still hard to hold on to that ox. It's still hard to maintain awareness of our true nature. We cling to our delusion of our separateness. We cling to our personal self. Our conditioning is strong. We have a sense of freedom, connection, and expansiveness, and then we lose it.

We still have our conditioning and attachments to deal with. It's why we practice—because it's easy to lose that sense of spaciousness and, with it, a sense of joy and belonging. So we practice. Regularly. When the ox heads into the mountains and the mist, we come back to practice.

Our conditioning and habits of separateness are not gone, but as we practice, they move to the background. Into the foreground comes a sense of fundamental connection with everything around us—instead of the other way around. We still have images of ourselves and others, but we begin to see through them. We see that the image is, well, an image.

This stage says, you throw a rope around it, but it will pull away. It's not easy to make it your own. One way to work with this experience is to do what a priest Shichiri Osho advised his monks: He suggested it was like holding beans in your mouth: You don't spit them out and you don't swallow them.

"Hold the beans always in your mouth," he taught.

What is he saying? He is saying maintain mindful attention. Holding the beans in your mouth is a way to keep your awareness, always. You don't spit them out. You don't swallow them. You keep your edge in terms of your practice. In the Zendo, we train the mind. When we leave the Zendo, we practice that training in our life.

I've shared this story before, but it seems pertinent. A long time ago, at a weeklong sesshin with Roshi Kennedy, we were having lunch, and he got up and served everyone coffee or tea or whatever they needed. Table by table with silent attention, he served all who wanted anything. They were him. He was them. He just served. I thought, well, he is the teacher for me because he's practicing the Way in the world. He is practicing what he has realized.

He was a little bit like Shichiri Osho, keeping the beans in his mouth. Because the ox can so easily get away, disappearing into the misty mountains.

Daido Loori writes that after the original breakthrough of seeing our true nature, wisdom can begin to function. When the mind connects to the heart, wisdom starts to unfold. We have the mind in unity with the heart of wisdom that opens us.

I loved seeing my teacher serving others. Just picking up the coffeepot. Walking around to each table. Decaf or regular? What do you need? What would you like? This is determination and intimacy. Now, I'm sure, just like the rest of us, he fell into his own ignorance and arrogance at times, his own persistent desires. I'm sure that the ox disappeared for him, too. But he kept practicing.

The moment of insight for me was very interesting. I was in the Zendo in Jersey City, sitting and working on koans, and I passed the koan "*Mu.*" It was as if a bright light started shining on all things. I went outside laughing like a fool, happy, because everything I saw was me. The maple trees were me. The gray clouds were me. The couple arguing on the street was me. The migrant cutting someone's lawn was me. The homeless person going through the garbage was me. There was no other. I felt a great freedom and belonging. That's why we practice, to see that, live that.

Now, you cannot hold on to that insight either. If you try to do that, you are stuck in the same boat again. We see it, we feel it, we try to experience it through our practice, but we know that we are going to lose it so we practice again. We lose it again, and we practice again. We practice keeping the beans in our mouth.

> *Through extraordinary effort, you seize the ox.*
> *Still, its will is forceful, and its body is spirited.*
> *Sometimes, it runs high into the mountains,*
> *other times, it disappears into the mist.*

Remarks on "Faith in Mind"

Good evening. I've been reading the sutra "Faith in Mind." Sometimes it's called "Faith Mind," sometimes "Faith Heart-Mind," sometimes "Verses on the Faith Mind."

I find it to be such an important text. This work is attributed to the Third Patriarch, Seng-Ts'an, who died in AD 606. Of course, it's difficult to know if that is historically accurate. Nevertheless, it's a wonderful guide and teaching and its value is in the message.

The word *Mind* in the title is very important. True faith in mind is the realization that we all have what we call Buddha Mind. It is fundamental. It is unchanging. It is not the mind we usually talk about and experience. It is not the thinking ego-mind or small mind. In "Faith in Mind," Seng-Ts'an shows us how to transform ordinary mind into a mind that isn't caught up in dualistic thinking about this and that, likes and dislikes.

It is important to understand that there is no *"true Buddha Mind"* that we have to *"get."* Buddha Mind, or what we sometimes call Big Mind, just IS. There is nothing to attain. Through this poem, we see that the teaching is more about the practice of equanimity.

I want to read a section that speaks to what I feel is the crux of the work for our practice, the hard work of the practice:

The Way is perfect, like vast space where nothing is lacking and nothing is in excess. Indeed, it is due to our choosing to accept or reject that we do not see the true nature of things. Live neither in the entanglements of outer things, nor in inner feelings of emptiness. Be serene in the oneness of things and such erroneous views will disappear by themselves. When you try to stop activity to achieve passivity, your very effort fills you with activity. As

101

long as you remain in one extreme or the other, you will never know the Oneness of things. Those who do not live in this single way fail in both activity and passivity, assertion and denial. To deny the reality of things is to miss their reality.

As I sat with this passage, one line in particular struck me: *When you try to stop activity to achieve passivity, your very effort fills you with activity.* All the striving, all the effort to achieve something, creates exactly the opposite of what you intended. I think this is where our work really is. It's hard work, difficult to do.

A fundamental teaching of Zen is that things as they are, are the Way, and the Way is perfect in this moment, right now. In every moment we encounter, in every moment we experience, Buddha Mind lacks nothing. You are perfect as you are right now.

But, that shouldn't be understood as meaning I don't have to keep working on my character. We work on returning to that perfection because, as we all know, desires pull us away from realization. We are perfect, yet as Suzuki Roshi wrote, we still need to work on improving our character.

This is a difficult idea to get and hang out and be with. It is hard to take it in in a real way. We hear it and think about it, but I have the sense that we don't really trust this teaching of original perfection. We're conditioned to focus on either our deficits or our excesses. Too much of this, not enough of that, and how we're not good enough and how we should be. We find more value in controlling than in trusting. However, practice, and the "Faith in Mind" poem, tell us we have to trust ourselves. If you really want to know who you are, the Buddha said, you have to find out for yourself. Do not fundamentally trust what you're told. Then you'll know the truth. The teachings in the Zen tradition say the same thing: Know who you are through your own practice and your own realization in your own way with your own style through your own experience.

The teachings remind us of that. They're like guardrails—but we need to verify them with our experience, not hold them blindly or rigidly. They should be confirmed through our own body, mind, life, activity, and practice. Trust the teachings, but only if you can apply them and if they make sense and resonate in your life.

Take, for example, the teaching that it is possible for us to be freer and suffer less. How do we apply that? The way to do that, "Faith in Mind" tells us, is not to attach. That's a great teaching. I want to have faith in the teaching that if I don't attach, that is the pathway to be freer. That includes our thoughts, our emotions, our reactivity, and our conditioning; our desires, greed, jealousy, and anger are all hindrances, the Buddha said, and can prevent us from experiencing that sense of freedom and the lessening of suffering. Yet, when we acknowledge and work with those hindrances, they are transformed into pathways for liberation. If we see the things that make us suffer and take a close look at them, if we welcome and explore them, those very barriers become the path. In the psychotherapy world, we say, "*The problem is the solution.*"

That we can transform our situation, that we can actually transform it, is an act of faith. Whatever your problem, when you hang out with it, when you are curious rather than condemning and are willing to look at and through it, and see what it's about, it becomes a pathway. This is what Seng-Ts'an means by faith in mind. The work is inside. Seeing how we get caught in greed, anger, fear, jealousy, desire, and attachments, seeing how these things block the sense of awareness we want for ourselves—just seeing it, in an open and friendly way—is the work of Zen practice. We look at it, we talk about it, but on a day-to-day basis, it can be hard to do. These things are entrenched in us.

The Great Way is not difficult, the poem says, just don't pick and choose. In your zazen, when you notice the beginning of picking and choosing, "I like this and I don't like that. I want this, not that" you just breathe it out. You let preferences go. We notice and release and come back to Big Mind, Buddha Mind—an open consciousness that has no preference for one state over another. It is an open embrace of our experience. We trust the teaching that the very hindrance I'm noticing—if I hang out with it, if I don't attach to it but see through it—is a pathway.

The Gatha of Atonement speaks about greed, anger, and ignorance—the three poisons. But when you explore greed, it turns into generosity. When you face your ignorance, it transforms into wisdom. When you investigate anger, it changes into compassion. By working with the poisons, they become the three wholesome attitudes. If you go back to some of the work of Carl Jung on mythology, he would say, "You've got to kiss the frog." Because when you kiss it, it transforms, and so do we. We have a picture in my house of a frog with a little crown on his head. The frog is the prince or princess. If you want to meet the prince or princess, you've got to kiss the frog. That's where it is. It's not about stopping any activity or withdrawing from the world.

I spoke recently about challenging the tendency, when we're sitting in zazen, to make ourselves a blank slate. The mind should be active, investigating the nature of things and working with them. Even though we're sitting, zazen is not a passive practice. We're not retreating from the world. We're engaging it in a new and interesting way, with curiosity and great love, actually, in order to see what blocks our awareness of the teaching that we are perfect and complete, that we lack nothing right from the very beginning. Holding on to that belief and trusting in it, you explore what gets in the way of your realizing it.

That's a cool thing to do, and it is worth the work. But you can't skip over the barrier. You must be willing to see it and untangle it so that the barrier becomes a path.

Just kiss the frog.

§

Roshi: I'd be curious about your thoughts about this. Exploring this piece is such an important aspect of what we do in terms of Zen, and so hard to do. Sensei Alice, do you have a comment or a thought you want share with us?

Sensei Alice: I spontaneously thought, "Bring on that frog. Bring on the frog!" And it touched me when you referred to the beauty, if I heard what you said, the beauty of these teachings. Just the beauty of them. And the promise in Zen, that yes, you can be free and suffer less. That it's not just an empty promise, and if you sit long enough, perhaps you will experience that. No—we all do and we all will experience it. It is our birthright almost.

Roshi: Not even almost. It is. But we do have to do some work to actualize it.

Sensei Alice: So, bring on that frog. We are perfect, but there is room for improvement in perfection. I'm perfect at any moment, but I'm not complete. And that's also beautiful. There's no bottom to it. That's the work that you described. Thank you.

Roshi: Thank you, Alice.

Student: I was thinking that one way I work with this is to use the word *soften*. I soften into things that I'm resistant to. So, if I'm on the cushion and I'm resistant, I soften my body. And if I soften my attitude, it can help me if I'm in anger or aversion or something like that.

Softening helps me be with whatever's there, which to me is like trying to kiss the frog.

Roshi: Yes, I like what you're saying, because there is implicit in this a sense of trust, right? I trust that if I soften, if I open, something can change. Something can be revealed that is not going to be revealed by hardness, but by kind of opening up to it. And I think that's wonderful. It's a nice way to put it.

Student: I liken my meditation practice to my yoga practice. I can be in a posture and not move, but I'm engaged—there's action, there's intention there. It's not visible, but I can feel it. Holding out my arm, I can hold it and let it be there, or I can engage the muscles. And it's a very different experience. And I think it's the same kind of approach with meditation.

Roshi: I've described it as being like a spinning top: There's activity in the stillness. There's activity in the mind, the same way you're engaged in your yoga posture. You take the warrior pose, and there's no outer movement, but there's engagement in a wider way. I think this is the grit of our practice, which is why I wanted to speak about it. I would like to encourage all of us to look at this, because it goes against what we've learned. We've learned to get away, to get some ice cream. I'm going to go play tennis. I'm going to watch a movie. Or we write a whole novel about our suffering, you know? We can go to these excesses, one or the other, rather than seeing them and saying hello to them, and releasing to see what's there and what they have to teach us. This is the grit of the work I'd like to encourage all of us to do. Maybe we'll do a study of "Faith in Mind." I would suggest that you pick it up and read it. There are a number of nice translations. Any last thought, question, comment, insight, a sharing of your experience? How is this working for you?

Student: I seem to want to add that seeing perfection in everything is a starting point, and that my efforts to change something are also perfect. Part of the perfection, so I'm not stuck with some static thing I have to swallow and choke on, if you know what I mean.

Roshi: That's right. I do. You want to grow, to be free, right? To realize freedom is not to go charging ahead as if we didn't already have it. As they say, the more you seek something, the farther away from it you become. The premise is that we already have it, so where are we going to seek it? So, it's more about the method we use to realize it. You don't have to go anywhere. You just look down and in and through your experience to let it teach you, because it's already there.

Student: I want to note how early we make a connection between imperfection and love. I think we learn at a very young age that when we do something bad, we're not lovable. I have a four-year-old grandson, and the other day, he was naughty. Then it passed, and we were walking back to the dinner table, and he said, "Baba, do you hate me when I'm bad?" And I said, "No, of course not. And I think you know that."

It strikes me how early we learn that imperfection and being unlovable are one and the same. Being soft, you know, as the student said, putting space around all of that, allows things to arise without judging them. Then the imperfection goes away.

Roshi: Thank you. The other side of this is also true— which is to know the difference between exploration and license to do what you want. If I'm perfect and everything is perfect, then I can do what I want, which is rather adolescent. That's why I think the word *attachment* is so important. It's not like you can just do whatever you want. The practice is to see where you're hooked because that hook is the block from the realization that you're whole and complete, lacking nothing from the beginning.

So, we look at the hindrances. You can't jump them. You have to look through them. But it doesn't mean you can do whatever you want. That's the other trap. Thank you. It's great. We can keep working with this because it's one of the biggest sticking points in terms of the teaching of how to be free.

Joshu's Dog

Welcome, everyone. A fundamental teaching in Zen Buddhism is "*just this*" —or the "*isness*" of things. What I mean by that is the awareness, beyond our particular projections and views, that this world is absolutely perfect as it is. Although our particular lives may be messy, our teachings tell us that underneath that mess (or more accurately, *as* that mess), we are alright. We are still after all, Buddha. Even our difficulties and messy lives are Buddha. Buddhism teaches that all is one—nothing is excluded. Life presents us with endless opportunities to wake up.

If we are able to realize this, not just logically but intuitively, it changes how we live. There is an inner clarity that can help us as we work through the struggles. Dogen expressed this as "*All beings and things are Buddha nature.*"

This takes me to the first great koan in *The Gateless Gate*, "Joshu's Dog." This koan is usually the first one a student encounters in koan study. It's considered the first gate of Zen to enter.

A monk, in all earnestness, asks Joshu, "*Does a dog have Buddha nature or not?*" And Joshu says, "*Mu!*" (No).

In his preface, Mumon, who compiled *The Gateless Gate,* wrote:

The great way is gateless.
Approached in a thousand ways.
Once past this checkpoint,
You stride freely through the universe.

For me, this koan was a high mountain to climb, until one day I realized it was more about descending a mountain than climbing one. What I mean is to come down from all my high-minded intellectual ideas about the koan. Descending, for me, meant not-knowing as opposed to "*I have to know*" or "*I should know.*" Descent, as Joseph Campbell said, is the beginning of wisdom. When we are free of the idea that we must know, we are better able to connect with the vastness of this life, so something new can touch us. Life beyond our thoughts can touch us. Joshu takes all the knowing away from this earnest young monk and drops him into not-knowing when he says "NO!" The monk must have been very confused as I'm sure all his learning was that everything has Buddha nature. Joshu is not interested in that idea. He wants to take those notions away so the young fellow can make contact with reality.

As I sat in zazen with this koan I remembered a picture on a wall when I visited Bernie Glassman in Yonkers. The picture was of a dog standing up on his back legs against a gate. There was no fence just a freestanding gate in an open field. Yet it seems the dog can't enter even though it wants to and it's a wide-open space. I often felt just like this dog approaching this first koan. So, the dog, of course, is us. [laughter]

About this, Maezumi Roshi said, "*Now once through the gate, we make the discovery that the gate is not a barrier in which to pass. It's simply reality presenting itself.*" Usually, we think of a gate as a barrier that stops us from going further. But Maezumi is pointing to a state where there is no coming or going. The commentary in the koan goes on:

> "*To attain this subtle realization, you must completely cut off thinking. If you don't pass the barrier, and do not cut off your thinking, then you're going to be like a ghost, clinging to bushes and weeds.*" An endless number of students have asked, "Well, if I am Buddha nature, perfect and complete, lacking nothing, then why do I suffer so much? Why do I feel like a dog sometimes?"

But in this koan, Joshu is not trying to help him solve this dilemma. He is trying to help him get out of the misunderstanding altogether. So, Joshu says, *"Mu."* But it isn't a *"no"* as, in, *"No, a dog doesn't have Buddha nature."* The *"no"* means *"Wrong question!"*

Joshu is saying, drop the dualistic thinking of yes and no. As the verse accompanying this koan teaches us: *"A moment of yes and no, lost are your body and soul."*

This koan is about realizing unity. The liminal—that which touches what is beyond personality. It is realizing that there is no separate, substantive self. Whatever we see is only made of every other thing. It is seeing the source behind or manifested as the 10,000 things. Or we might say the thusness of all things.

Another way to say this is that this life is one single endless tissue or net (think Indra's Net) but we recognize it as individual things. We usually do not realize the Oneness that makes each individual thing. This is what Joshu is attempting to help the young monk see.

We say Oneness is the experience of realizing the inter-connectedness of all things.

We practice to awaken to that fact. We practice open and remember a vast consciousness that is part of us. To re-connect to it.

I think it's true that we all want is what is pleasurable and hope to avoid what is not. We all have the tendency to move toward what is comfortable and keeps us feeling safe and away from what doesn't. All sentient beings do that, certainly dogs. We are still all Buddhas even when we act like dogs.

We all move toward love and comfort and away from pain.

We are beautiful, perfect Buddhas, and disagreeable, difficult, often unhappy Buddhas too.

Now, this idea of comfort is important because comfort usually means the same experience. It means staying within the realm of what is repetitive. We have habits that make us comfortable. We have set views that make us feel comfortable. But life itself is not repetitive. It is always new and changing. It takes stepping out of our comfort zone to awaken. One quality we speak of often is curiosity. One small example of this is when I stepped outside one day listening to the calls of birds. But suddenly my ears perked up and I came to attention on hearing a new sound. I opened to a new awareness rather than the familiar sounds of morning birds. That's why we say, meditation is not about blissing out or falling into unconsciousness, where we repeat those same old familiar ways of seeing and thinking about the world. As life is always new, when we try to hold on to our set ways and thoughts, we suffer. Life is actually always tapping us on the shoulder. We just have to have a mind that is open to it.

Practice is difficult and requires effort and rigor. We teach that the practice of zazen is not blissing out. It requires attention, so we work not only with positive emotions that arise but also the afflictive ones. We don't get rid of anything! What we do, though, is develop the capacity to be present to our life in a way that goes beyond just thinking or rationalizing about it. In other words, we develop a skill to see beyond the cloud of our interpretations, commentaries, conceptual thinking, and reactions.

When we come to the zendo and to practice together we are really longing to return home. To realize our home is here. Now. Actually, wherever we are is home. We don't have to do or be someone special. Practicing in this way opens us to that bigger consciousness I mentioned earlier. If we practice with diligence, attention and a generous spirit that notion of a separate self can start to fall away. You may have the realization that unlike that dog in the picture, you can walk through or around the gate of the small thinking mind.

We can begin to see that everything we do is that bigger awareness operating in our life. The bowing, the chanting. The same is true when we leave the zendo and go home. We ask, what is *Mu*? Well, it's the action of cleaning the bathroom. Of walking and talking and being.

It's just that we lose our relationship to that larger consciousness. Our practice helps us realize that. So, to stop and look at our life as it is without complaint is the beginning of kindness. We see that if we don't, our heart clenches and turns cold. I don't think anyone of us gets rid of our conditioned ways of being easily. They are part of our history and well-oiled habits. But if we can bear them, embrace them as best we can, then our heart opens. Actually, when we are kind, even to our flaws and mistakes, we can more easily work to soften them. What I mean by work with them is that we drop the notion of having to be perfect. When we do that, it is easier to look at them and change our behavior, even if we can't change our conditioning.

I think that is our work. We are perfect and far from perfect at the same time as Suzuki Roshi wrote. So, we practice and remain alert, attentive, and humble. We drop the idea of Buddha nature and no Buddha nature. We drop our attachment to all opposites and instead just see and accept what is in front of us moment after moment.

When we don't look at all aspects of our life and rest in kindness for all of it, we are not free but are caught up too much in our own purpose, point of view. Pursuing our likes and trying to push away our dislikes. Operating this way makes our heart clench.

113

In our practice of zazen, we don't expect anything. We let go of trying to achieve anything. Instead, we become the situation or experience we're having. Of course, it is natural to have thoughts and concepts, but in our spiritual practice, we don't give them much value. As I mentioned earlier when we practice what I call a radical acceptance of ourselves, all aspects of our experience and ourselves, we open into a larger awareness.

One Bright Pearl

Good evening. I'm happy to be here to offer a few words tonight. I've been thinking a lot about what it means to be here and to live this life fully alive! I have been asking myself the question: How do you want to live this fleeting life?

Perhaps I'm thinking about this because I'm in my 70s now. I'm painfully aware there is more time behind me than in front of me. Also, perhaps like me, some of you hear more and more stories each day of friends and loved ones who have either left or passed away. I see these stories and the reality of this fleeting life as a doorway to consider how I want to use my time. I ask myself, as in a koan: What matters?

The way I see it, our entire spiritual practice is simply to answer that question. How do we make use of this life we have? I don't think life is about us sculpting it to what we want. Life is not interested in what we want. It gives us a path to take. To think that life should give us what we want is a prescription for not living very well. Instead, I suggest appreciating what is right in front of us. I think this is why we practice together, to appreciate our life. I would say, to enjoy the life we have. Sometimes we can take practice too seriously. We forget the joy. When we sit zazen, we should be explorers not just for peace or contentment but also to reconnect to a sense of joy.

When my granddaughter was young, she would help my wife and me reconnect to that. One time we went to her house and she said, *"Do you know what I found today? My favorite ribbon!! It's red!!"* I don't think that sense of wonder is only a child's realm.

I know we speak of this so often, but it needs saying. How do we rekindle this childlike openness and curiosity for our life? It means paying attention, which allows us the experience of joy or perhaps equanimity. Another way to think and work with this is to pause. Just to stop and look. But look deeply. I do think our practice of zazen has that quality of helping us to pause.

In our pausing, we open the door to recover presence of mind even when we are disappointed or discontent. At our Zendo, we sometimes ask the question: How do we use the difficulties that arrive to help us be more awake? Well, aren't great difficulties also the dharma?

It's not that we want great difficulties, but they show up, don't they? So, what will you do? We need an awareness or consciousness that embraces the hard times as well without losing our balance, or perhaps allowing us to return to balance a bit more quickly.

I went searching for a koan that might speak to this and found one from the great Zen teacher Gensha.

> Gensha, the son of a poor fisherman, watched his father get washed away and die in a river during a spring flood. Heartbroken and confused, he sought refuge in a monastery—a place he thought might help him find peace. But he couldn't find it even in a monastery. After a few years, he left to wander in the mountains, hoping to understand what it was the sages who seemed at peace in their lives had found. He hadn't gone far when his foot struck a sharp rock. It was painful—his foot was wounded, there was blood. But from the shock of the pain, he suddenly understood what the sages had found and he had been seeking. He realized the entire world was this one moment. Here. Now. This. Just this. His sense of who he was and wanted to be disappeared. He discovered that the world was one single reality with no size, or space, no past, no future, no plan he could rely on. In becoming aware of that singleness, he experienced an open heart toward everything, including his life experiences. Including the time in the mountains and the pain in his foot. And he felt a profound sense of peace and joy.

All along, he thought to himself, I have been carrying around the treasure I've been seeking. Only it was not a thing among other things. Instead, it was every last thing within itself. He himself was none other than that very treasure.

Overjoyed—despite the pain in his foot—he went back down the mountain to the monastery. The master asked, "*You're back so soon. What happened?*"
Gěnsha replied, "*I never took a single step. The whole universe is one bright pearl!*"

How beautiful is that? That is how I want to see and move in my world, too. This entire universe without exception is one bright pearl that we have always had with us. There's another short koan that is along these lines:

> *A student asked his teacher, "What about all the chaos?"*
> *And the teacher said, "That's it, too."*

We have to make a conscious effort to open up mind and heart to what life gives us. To raise our awareness and rely on our practice, to trust our practice and teachings like this one when—not if—great difficulties come.

Everything is one bright pearl. It is hard to believe, isn't it? This is why we practice. To question our old narratives and beliefs. To do this, we need a regular practice, and teachers we can trust, and a community of our sangha mates. I would like to encourage everyone to see how we can apply this one bright pearl teaching in our lives. It is available to us all.

Zen Training, Zen Practice

I want to talk about the difference between training and practice. There is a fundamental difference between them. The Zendo is a training space where we train the mind; this training is fundamentally about transforming our consciousness. It's also a space for transforming how we move in relationships both in the world and our personal lives. But the training is here.

Let us call it mind training. Each thing we do in the Zendo is fundamentally about first being aware of what is needed. Whether we're lighting incense or bowing, we're developing a mindset of awareness. Then we take it home. When people first come to the Zendo, they come thinking or believing that they are here just for themselves. That's okay. That is how we start.

We think we're just coming for ourselves, that we're coming just to sit. Then, after a while, if we are lucky, we realize that we're sitting with others, that we're part of a community. We're not just sitting here ourselves.

We come to sit with a community of practitioners, and we grow in that practice with each other. If we're lucky, down the road, we start realizing that we are sitting not with others, but for others. That our own awakening, our own awareness, our own growth and spiritual maturity affect everyone. How I think, how I move in the world, how I see relationships, affects everybody. So, we don't just sit for ourselves. We sit for each other. That's very, very important to get. That is spiritual maturity.

If we are oblivious to these things in the Zendo, we are oblivious to them at home. The root of being oblivious is self-centeredness, thinking that you're moving alone in the world, on your own, by yourself and for yourself and that nothing you do affects anyone or anything but you. Here we are training to become not self-centered but multi-centered. Training to see that what I do and do not do directly affects who you are, what you do, and how you function. Thich Nhat Hanh called this *interbeing*.

That is what's happening here or should be happening here if we're doing our job of training the mind and training our behavior and conduct, our way of moving in the world so we're not oblivious, not just going about bumping into things throughout the day thinking it's all about us. It's important to get that, to understand that. That's why we focus so much on being of service.

You can call it skillful means. Skillful means is skillfully applying what we learn here in our world. Make no mistake; this is a training center for the mind, for awakening the mind. All the practices we do are about that.

We had a session last weekend culminating on Sunday with the installation of a new teacher, Henry Fersko-Weiss. He's going to be a teacher. He's solid. Good character, good insight. I gave him the name Myoshin, which means, *"illuminated heart-mind."* Myoshin.

During the installation ceremony, we recited the names of all the teachers who have gone before. We named the Indian, Chinese, and Japanese patriarchs, and the Americans, and then the matriarchs. All of the wisdom women who were either neglected or forgotten in the past. We made sure to name every one of the forty of them.

All of those who went before us. I was thinking as we were reading their names that these were actual men and women who practiced as we do now. They struggled as we struggle and lost their way as we lose ours, and some found their way back and became teachers. None of them were perfect enlightened human beings, just human beings who were deeply curious, had some kind of awakening and wanted to serve others.

Hundreds and hundreds of years of teachers from all around the world. We're lucky that they left us their teachings, and a path for us to follow. How beautiful is that? As we were reading their names, something else fell away for me, another layer of the illusion of separation: I realized that all those teachers are here. Right here, now, in the Zendo. They sat and sit with us now. We bring them alive when we sit well.

We bring them to life because we are following their teachings. I kept looking over at the teacher table. Maezumi Roshi, Roshi Robert Kennedy, Bernie Glassman Roshi, Yamada Roshi. We could put so many more up there.

I like to say, *life is out to get us—to wake up. To break us open. Life is always trying to do that.*

I thought about the sound of the bell, which asks us to wake up. To pay attention. Peter rang the bell for the installation ceremony. Man, he rang the bell. When Peter McRobbie rings the bell, you know that bell is rung. There is no holding back when Peter rings the bell.

Something's happening! Pay Attention!

If you are zoning out and oblivious and you hear the bell, it pulls you right back. We use the bell, but to open the mind, it can be any sound: a child laughing, a car rushing by, birdsong, a siren. When we start to transform the mind and open it, all sounds become skillful means to help us awaken. If we are oblivious, if we are zoning out, they call us back to the moment. One thing we're doing here is training the mind so it doesn't take us five years to realize that life is calling us back.

During a practice circle recently, someone said, *"Oh my God, what did I do with my life? What have I done? Why didn't somebody tell me this before?"* One teacher has called it an available secret, which I think is really interesting. It's not well known, but at the same time, it's always available. We're cultivating a mindset in zazen that makes the secret more available. That is a beautiful thing. An available secret. We can unlock it. We unlock it through practice.

In training the mind, you start to see the barriers we create that keep us oblivious and self-centered. The barriers that we have erected or that have been told to us that we've come to believe, that stop us from feeling and connecting to life as fully as we can. You start to recognize this through zazen.

Even your belief system, even your delusions, are a bell that can wake you up if you know how to work with them, explore them. Or as I like to say, be curious about them. That's pretty cool, isn't it? That our problems become some of our greatest teachers. So, the sound of the bell made me think about Basho's great haiku:

> *An ancient pond*
> *A frog jumps in*
> *The sound of water*

And...

> *The temple bell stops ringing,*
> *but the sound keeps reverberating*
> *out of the flowers.*
> *Where is the end of it?*

In meditation, sometimes that experience of separation, of subject and object falls away or blurs. Whatever you see, is you. You see a crow, and you can feel its wings. The call of the bird is your call, and you are singing it. The child is laughing in the street, and you feel it inside.

When I was studying with Roshi Kennedy, He asked me in daisan, *"Who are you?"* And I said, *"I'm a mountain."*

I had been hiking in the White Mountains in New Hampshire. I did that every year for a few years. I'd hike to the peaks, and at some point, I disappeared and my experience was that every mountain, tree, and stream was me. At some point, it was no longer me walking through the mountains. It was just the walking, the mountain, and the movement. It was just the sound, the hush of the wind across the peaks. An absolute blue sky.

He said, *"Say something else."* So, I started to dance and he gave me the dharma name *Ruzan*, *"Flowing Mountain,"* like the flow of a dance. And in hindsight, very appropriate. But my point here is, that's what we want to try to do through our training here. That's why we do sesshin. That's why we sit as much as we sit—to break through the barrier that the small mind has created, to open up into something greater and let life touch us and to *be* that.

That kind of consciousness, that kind of awakening, is available for us all the time. Whatever you see is you. The sound of the car, the sound of the bell, anything can wake us up if we are ready to receive it. That's why we train. Thank you.

Row, Row, Row Your Boat

Welcome, everyone. I woke up in the middle of the night last night, as I sometimes do when I'm going to give a talk. I have a little notepad on the nightstand in case a line of poetry comes, or something like that. After I wrote down some lines, I went back to sleep, and the next morning I didn't remember what I had written. It was as if it had been a dream. The four lines I'd written down were:

Row, row, row your boat,
gently down the stream,
merrily, merrily, merrily, merrily,
life is but a dream.

They were so startling in their profundity!
... *Life is but a dream.*

I thought, as I was driving here this morning "Well, that says it all!" I recalled Bernie Glassman giving a talk about that line and how it spoke to how we live this life.

In that moment, I felt grateful for all of you and all the teachers who have gone before who walked this path and passed their teachings on to us. I became aware of the opportunity that I have, and you have, to live a fuller, freer life because of their efforts. Though the stories have changed over time, and the words may have been rewritten, the koans and stories we study and talk about came from real people, men and women who walked the Way. They were not gods or deities; they were like you and me, struggling and practicing, as we do, to live a free, upright life, learning how to work with life's struggles.

It's the struggles that create the freedom— no struggle, no freedom. No struggle, no enlightenment. By struggle, I mean the discontent we feel about this life and how we live it.

The path to living a more joyful life begins with questioning the beliefs and plans we hold. What is that old phrase– We plan, God laughs. The struggles and the issues that we encounter during our life can be the grist for the mill of our awakening.

Somebody said to me the other day that people come to the Zendo for two reasons: the carrot or the stick. Either because they're here because they are suffering—the stick—or they want something more—the carrot. The real deal is to come to this practice and stay with it. To look deeply at the nature of our lives and the notions we hold that create suffering for us. We speak so often about the Buddha's teaching that we are whole and complete, yet as we go through our life, we lose that awareness. We have the opportunity here to ask ourselves what barriers we create by our own grasping, by wanting something different— they are the very nature of what causes us to suffer. It takes courage and effort to ask that question.

That brings me back to Row, Row, Row your boat. It's interesting to me, though, that in a sense we go against the stream. By this, I mean the stream of our culture and identity, which tell us in so many ways that we are not whole and complete that being happy is buying more and having more. That to be happy, we should fulfill all our desires. That culture doesn't address how to achieve a deeper, unconditioned happiness; it doesn't give out awards for equanimity!

We have the opportunity here to row down a different stream. The stream of our true nature, of our original perfection. When we let go of our attachments and row the boat we have, which is our life, enlightenment is waiting to happen.

In just rowing, there's nothing to hold on to; it's just rowing. Moment to moment, we guide the boat the best we can, carrying ourselves and caring for ourselves and others the best we can. We row the boat of our life and practice as skillfully as we can, navigating the stream of enlightenment that we're always on.

Row, row, row your boat,
gently down the stream,
merrily, merrily, merrily, merrily,
life is but a dream.

Ray Ruzan Cicetti, roshi, is the founder and senior teacher of the Empty Bowl Zen Community in Morristown, New Jersey. He grew up in Newark New Jersey, and graduated from Hunter College with a master's degree in social work. He worked in various mental health agencies before going into private practice. He began formal study in Zen with Roshi Robert Jinsen Kennedy in 1989 and received dharma transmission from him in 2004 and Inka in 2019. He is particularly interested in the relationship between Zen practice and the arts. He is the author of two books of poetry: *A Forest in His Pocket* (2020) (Finishing Line Press) and *Songs of Love & Longing* (2023) (Blue Jade Press) His poems have been published in a variety of journals including: *The Paterson Literary Review, The Galway Review, Deep Wild Journal, River Heron* and *The Stillwater Poetry Review.* He is also the author of the chapter, A Journey Toward Awakening in Self-Relations in Mindfulness in the book *Walking in Two Worlds* (Zeig, Tucker & Theisen) Ray lives with his wife Carolyn in northern New Jersey.

www.ingramcontent.com/pod-product-compliance
Lightning Source LLC
Chambersburg PA
CBHW071349090426
42738CB00012B/3067